THE PERFECT PICKLE BOOK

DAVID MABEY
AND
DAVID COLLISON

BBC BOOKS

This book accompanies the BBC television series
The Perfect Pickle Programme
produced by Third Eye Productions Ltd

ILLUSTRATED BY CHARLES STEWART

Published by BBC Books
A division of BBC Enterprises Ltd
Woodlands, 80 Wood Lane, London W12 0TT

First published 1988
© David Mabey and David Collison 1988
ISBN 0 563 21445 7

Reprinted 1990

Typeset in Itek Goudy
by Ace Filmsetting Ltd, Frome, Somerset
Printed in England by Clays Ltd, St Ives plc

CONTENTS

PREFACE
A Passion for Pickles by Davilia David   6

INTRODUCTION   8

1   THE HISTORY OF PICKLING   11

2   FIRST PRINCIPLES   15

3   THE ENGLISH TRADITION   23

4   NORTH & SOUTH AMERICA   71

5   THE CARIBBEAN   81

6   SCANDINAVIA & NORTHERN EUROPE   88

7   EASTERN EUROPE   101

8   THE MEDITERRANEAN   109

9   THE MIDDLE EAST   118

10   INDIA   125

11   THE FAR EAST   139

APPENDIX   153
Specialist shops   153
Producers and suppliers of pickles and preserves   156

INDEX   157

ACKNOWLEDGEMENTS

An enormous number of people helped us to make *The Perfect Pickle Programme* and this, the book of the series, and we would like to thank them all. Some provided us with detailed information and recipes, others simply spared the time to talk to us about pickles. We are grateful to everyone who allowed us to invade their homes, kitchens, restaurants and shops, often at very short notice. Without exception, they rose to the occasion and gave a great deal more than was expected of them.

First, there were the chefs and restaurateurs: Anna Hegarty of Anna's Place, London N1; Antonio Carluccio of the Neal Street Restaurant, London WC2; Phillip Harris of the Bahn Thai Restaurant, London W1; Henry Tan of The Equatorial, London W1; Ewa Quinn of the Gentry Restaurant, London W3; Mayblin Hamilton of the Plantation Inn, Leytonstone; Tim Reeson formerly of The Crown, Southwold; John and Patricia Hegarty of Hope End Country House Hotel, near Ledbury; John and Carole Evans of The Roebuck, Brimfield; Bernard and Carla Phillips of the Moorings Restaurant, Wells-next-the-Sea; Victoria and Michael Stephenson, formerly of Bradfield House, Bradfield Combust.

Shopkeepers and commercial pickle-makers also helped, in particular Sheila Elstone of Elstone's, Knutsford; Sue Elston of Humble Pie, Burnham Market; Barry Rogg; Dounne Moore; Mike Rhodes and Steve Nurse of the Cley Smokehouse; Marion Cartwright of Cartwright and Butler; Kirit and Meena Patak of Patak Spices; William and Guy Tullberg of Wiltshire Tracklements.

Others who deserve a very special mention include Colin Spencer, Lesley Downer, Joan Poulson, Margaret Borthwick, Saroj Bajpai, Tuddy Holles, Val Hall, Sybil Norcott and her colleagues from the Dunham Massey WI, Jill Barker and her team from the Mere and Over Tabley WI,

Yvonne Ellis, Gee Kilpatrick, Andrew and Mary Bosi, Cedric Sharpley and the stallholders of Bury Market.

This book owes its existence to its parent television series *The Perfect Pickle Programme*, which was first encouraged and subsequently commissioned by Roger Laughton, then Head of BBC Daytime Television, and by Peter Ridsdale-Scott, Editor, Independent Productions, BBC North-West.

Without the initial research and leg-work of Alexandra Collison neither series nor book would ever have happened. Thank you, Sandy!

Finally, thanks to Suzanne Webber, Jennie Allen and her staff, Cath Speight and Sarah Spalding at BBC Books, who put the book into shape with such speed and diligence. And thanks to Jane Blagden, knitwear designer, for creating the pickle sweater and braces.

Why don't they make pickled onions square,
Why are they always round?
When I put my fork into the jar
All I get out is the vinegar.
Grab 'em, stab 'em,
They're nowhere to be found,
Oh, why don't they make pickled onions square,
Why are they always round?

(Pantomime song)

5

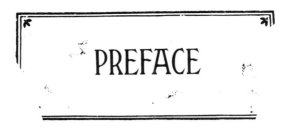

PREFACE

A PASSION FOR PICKLES

My first memory of pickles as a child in Australia is of a jar of pickled chillies my father had that were *his*. The red wrinkled pods stood drunkenly in their pale golden liquid and looked lethal. Whenever mother made a curry, the forbidden fruit were ceremoniously produced and we four girls watched in wonder as our father—now in the spotlight of attention—began to eat one or two of these fiery fingers, with only the slightest shudder to underline his bravery. To us it was a supreme manly deed of daring.

Pickled onions did not have the same forbidden attraction. My mother did not like them, so did not make them; she bought them sometimes, but they were nothing special. I discovered the real thing one day when I went to a school friend's house and found her father in the kitchen, up to his elbows in a sink surrounded by bobbing white globes. The air was heavy with the smell of onions, while from the stove came the fumes of spiced vinegar, which filled the room and almost took my breath away before they wafted out of the window. I could understand why mother didn't make them, but one taste of the real thing and I was hooked. They bore no resemblance to the shop-bought onions one found at parties in the city. When I went to dances in the country, however, there were always dishes of these crunchy, mouth-watering onions proudly placed with hams and turkeys on huge trestle tables laden with sherry trifles with proper custard and piled high with Jersey cream.

Domestic Science classes at my all-girls school were aimed at equipping young women for the running of rural outback homes. We learnt how to use flat irons from a wood stove, and how to clean them in sand and beeswax, much to our disdain, for we were city girls. But the classes did introduce me to my favourite basic cookbook, *The Golden Wattle Cookery Book*—every West Australian girl's domestic bible.

My home was often a hive of activity, preserving all the fruit and vegetables as they came into season. I will never forget the mulberry picking expeditions to two trees planted by early settlers on what was then common land. We would eat ourselves sick and come home covered with dark red sticky juice, bearing our billycans full of fruit for mother to bottle. At Christmas we often made presents of jams, jellies, mincemeat and sweets.

It was not until I came to England that I started to produce chutneys and pickles as presents for theatrical friends who, like me, were probably trying to fight the flab. There is often little or no sugar at all in pickles. Also, being an actress, I had limited funds and time on my hands due to gaps in employment.

It all started one autumn back in the sixties, when I had a load of home-grown green tomatoes. Not knowing what to do with them I got out my *Golden Wattle Cookery Book* and made my first batch of green tomato pickle. It was a great success, so I continued. Since then I have embarked on a magical mystery tour of the world's pickles, from the humble home-made pickled onion through Scandinavian cucumbers to blistering hot Indian and Caribbean peppers and chillies, which are shades of the forbidden fruit of my youth.

I have to admit that I prefer making other more interesting things (like my melon pickle) rather than pickling onions—but that's probably a good thing as I still think men make the best pickled onions. You should taste David Collison's shallots! David and I are amateur enthusiasts (often exchanging our latest creations), whereas David Mabey is our professional expert adviser. All three of us have a passion for pickles.

DAVILIA DAVID
May 1988

INTRODUCTION

We began our search for the perfect pickle in the Lancashire town of Bury. If the tradition of English pickle making was still alive, there would surely be signs of it here, among the black puddings, home-made pies and cheeses that have doggedly survived in this part of the North Country. And yes, as we trekked round the open market, we found all those famous regional specialities in abundance. But not a single home-made pickle. The only jars we did spot were from a pickle factory in Manchester—and they were tucked away at the back of the stalls or used to prop up displays of fine Lancashire cheese. The fact that we found no pickles wasn't simply disappointing. It was scandalous. A telling reminder of the way we so easily surrender some of our finest traditions in this careless country of ours.

What has happened? It seems that the art of pickling has been driven underground—or at least forced behind the kitchen door—over the last fifty years by the onward march of the food industry. There have been changes in fashion too, and people simply have less time to spare on such things. Everyone we talked to remembered their grandmother's pickles; a few had pickling parents; only a handful were gallantly carrying on the tradition because they loved it.

Delving a little deeper, we did find signs of life: in Knutsford there is Sheila Elstone making pickles as well as chutneys and marmalades for her greengrocer's shop; across the country in north Norfolk, Sue Elston runs an enterprising provisions shop and contracts local people to make pickles to supplement her own output. Above all, there are the ladies of the Women's Institutes, who have done more to protect and renew the traditions of home pickling than anyone else in England. In many ways they are the inheritors of a tradition that stretches back more than two centuries to great cooks and picklers such as Hannah Glasse and Elizabeth

Raffald. We have lost a great deal since then—not only in the range of pickles that now appear, but also in our dedication to the business and craft of pickling.

Pickles are also international, and we saw hundreds in our travels. What is astonishing is the sheer richness of the pickling tradition in many countries, and the fact that this tradition hasn't been whittled away. Even commercially produced pickles are generally of a very high quality, and above all, pickles are still regarded as an essential part of the larder. Two images stand out in our minds: the extraordinary array of nearly twenty different kinds of pickled wild mushrooms in the store room of the Neal Street Restaurant in Covent Garden. And then Phillip Harris of the Bahn Thai Restaurant in Soho, sitting behind a table laden with Thai pickles.

So, where are the new champions of English pickling? We found some of them, and there are two great hopeful signs. First the spawning of new cottage industries producing all kinds of pickles, preserves, condiments, maintaining their standards and resisting the temptation to sell-out to the big manufacturers. Secondly the revivalist trend in many British restaurants. Young chefs and restaurateurs are not only re-introducing pickles and preserves, but inventing completely new pickles for the eighties and nineties: Victoria Stephenson, until recently at Bradfield House, working with pickled asparagus and quails' eggs; John and Patricia Hegarty defending the English kitchen and the English garden at Hope End in Herefordshire, growing organically, and using pickles in wondrous ways; Tim Reeson, formerly of The Crown, Southwold, Suffolk, experimenting with pickled kohlrabi, spiced chicken and new ways of marinating raw fish in citrus juices.

Pickling is a great craft and trade. It doesn't need to be done out of necessity in this age of deep-freezes and refrigerators, which gives picklers the opportunity to use pickling as a way of creating new foods that can be preserved lightly and eaten within a few days in some cases. It is a new style, a new way of approaching this splendid domestic skill. Bury market is not the end of the story. Across the land there is a tremendous mood of enthusiasm. Make no mistake: pickles have a future.

Get pickling!

THE HISTORY OF PICKLING

People have been making pickles for more than 2000 years. It is one of the oldest methods of preserving food, although it doesn't have quite the same history as drying, salting and smoking. The earliest hunter-gatherers knew how to preserve their catch of meat and fish by drying it in the open air; Neolithic man worked out his own ways of curing long before the idea of pickling was discovered.

The Egyptians probably did some pickling; the Greeks certainly did, but it was the Romans who turned it into a fine art. Columella didn't mince words when he wrote 'vinegar and hard brine are essential for making preserves'. Vinegar meant 'sour wine', and that's exactly what it was made from in Roman times. Yeast, dried figs, salt and honey were added to produce something not only vital for pickling, but also used as a drink diluted with water.

The sheer range of Roman pickles was astonishing. Thanks to their vast empire and conquered territories they had access to almost every fruit, vegetable, spice and herb then known and cultivated: from North Africa and the Middle East came plums, lemons, peaches and apricots; from Europe came cured meats and vegetables; their own gardens produced a whole range of herbs, roots and flowers. There were recipes for pickled onions, plums, lettuce leaves, asparagus, fennel and cabbage stalks. Turnips were preserved in a pickle made from honey, myrtle berries and vinegar. The Roman way was to macerate the ingredients in a mixture of oil, brine and vinegar, which was added carefully drop by drop; then the pickles were stored for months in large cylindrical vases.

The Roman Empire didn't last, and after the fall, the centres of civilised cookery in Europe were the monasteries. The monks knew all about provisions. They made cheese, brewed beer, kept bees and were avid picklers, making extensive use of the produce from their herb and vegetable gardens and orchards. By the eleventh century most of these monastic skills had re-appeared in the kitchens of grand households. Pickling was probably quite limited during this period, because there were few vegetables available—onions, leeks, cabbages and some root crops, but very little else. Not a great prospect for anyone interested in pickling. Some produce was dried, but usually it was a question of eating what was fresh and in season. One of the few early references to a specific pickle is a recipe for 'pickled greens' in a household list of 1290. These were probably cabbages and they were most likely pickled in verjuice—the juice extracted from sour crab apples. (The word was used in Roman times to describe a kind of grape juice, but from the Middle Ages until the sixteenth century it was specifically made from crab apples.) It was rather like a very mild, sharp cider, which gives us a clue to the flavour and character of many of those early pickles.

During the sixteenth and seventeenth centuries, the list of fruits, vegetables and herbs available to cooks increased. And so did the number of pickles. This was pickling's first Golden Age, and it had its champions—all men: Gervaise Markham, Robert May, John Evelyn, whose *Acetaria* of 1699 is the great work of its time on herbs and salad vegetables. Here were recipes for pickling broom buds, alexander buds, rock samphire, ash keys, elder shoots, the leaves from young radishes, turnips and lettuce, as well as mushrooms, walnuts and cucumbers.

The Elizabethans loved colour, style and vividness in all things. In their great houses, food was presented with consummate care. Most dazzling of all was the grand salad or salmagundi—an extravagant array of all kinds of herbs, wild plants and vegetables, some raw, others boiled, often with cold meats, cured fish, hard-boiled eggs and a great assortment of pickled things as embellishments. It was also the fashion to decorate these dishes with fresh *and* pickled flowers to add a special colour and scent. The flamboyance, wit and whimsy of these great presentations matched perfectly the mood of the times.

The second Golden Age of pickling belonged exclusively to the ladies. By the middle of the eighteenth century, the first in a line of classic English recipe books was being published. These books covered every aspect of cooking and domestic skills, which naturally included pickling. Each had a substantial section devoted to the subject, with some marvellous recipes. Hannah Glasse, Eliza Smith, Elizabeth Raffald, Mrs Rundell and many others were the culinary heroines of their age, a century before Mrs Beeton laid her famous tome before the public.

There were echoes of the Elizabethan Age in many of these eighteenth-century pickles: recipes for radish pods, two ways of pickling artichokes (one using the young leaves, the other making use of the bottoms), barberries, fennel, alongside onions, beetroot and red cabbage. By this time, the range of fruits available to cooks had increased and many of these were pickled too: redcurrants and grapes, melons and peaches, often done in a liquor of wine or wine vinegar.

What really changed the face of pickling was the influence of the East India Company's trade with the Orient. Travellers brought back all kinds of exotica, from soy sauce to mangoes. This started a vogue for imitations: marrows were pickled to resemble mangoes; cauliflower stalks were turned into mock ginger and pickled elder shoots were thought to resemble bamboo shoots. Piccalilli also appeared around the beginning of the eighteenth century. The first recipes say 'To pickle lila, an Indian pickle.' Even then it was a vinegar-based sauce flavoured with garlic, mustard seeds, ginger and turmeric with pieces of cabbage, cauliflower and plums. Not very different to the bright yellow concoction that has become one of today's best-sellers.

From the east also came chutneys and ketchups. The word chutney is from the Hindustani *chatni*, meaning a strong sweet relish. Ketchup derived from the Chinese *koe-chiap*, a pickled fish sauce that was introduced into South East Asia and India by travellers and Chinese immigrants. So-called 'store sauces' became all the rage. There were powerful condiments made from anchovies, wine, horseradish and spices that were intended 'for the captains of ships'; there was Harvey's Sauce, Pontac Sauce made from elderberries and, in due course, the most famous of them all, Worcestershire Sauce. What they had in common was pungency and a potent spiciness. The same was true of pickles, which had developed a much stronger flavour than their Elizabethan counterparts.

By the middle of the nineteenth century many of the great pickles had disappeared, banished by lack of interest and changes in fashion. In 1845, when Eliza Acton published *Modern Cookery for Private Families*, the first commercial pickle factories had begun to appear in London. But Eliza was prepared to speak her mind: she was a champion of good home-cooking and proper pickles. Her book is full of precise, accurate observations and instructions, and she was not afraid to attack bad practice: she took the pickle makers to task for adulterating their vinegar (which was often composed of a dilute solution of sulphuric acid, coloured with burnt sugar), for deliberately making pickles in copper vessels so that they looked vivid green, but were potentially deadly; and she was prepared to say that most commercial pickles at that time were made from crude, hard, unripe fruit and were basically unwholesome. That was heady stuff for its day. No wonder Eliza Acton is now rated as the forerunner of modern cookery writers.

Since then, things appear to have improved. The food industry began to tighten up its standards, encouraged by laws which resulted from a special government enquiry into food adulteration in 1899. Successive bouts of legislation have attempted to safeguard the consumer, and 'quality control' is now the pickle makers' watchword. But what would Eliza Acton think of the onions from today's pickle factories, with their spirit vinegar, preservative E223, artificial sweeteners, caramel and colourings? And what would be her verdict on some of today's chutneys, with their sugar beet and swede, their modified starch and gum arabic and their bland, sickly sweet flavour? And what would she make of the dismal choice, centred around five or six old favourites? Pickles and chutneys are now big business. According to a survey produced by Crosse & Blackwell in 1987, the pickle and sauce market is worth £104 million per year and growing all the time. We may not be a nation of pickle makers, but we are certainly a nation of pickle eaters.

Alongside all the high-profile marketing of the food companies, a new spirit and interest in home-pickling is starting to gain ground. Right across the country there are scores of revivalist cottage industries making pickles on more than a domestic scale, but with real passion and enthusiasm. Their products won't replace the big names, but at least we now have some alternatives; old pickles are being re-discovered, new recipes are being invented. And in many enterprising restaurant kitchens, cooks and chefs are putting pickles back where they belong, right at the heart of British cooking.

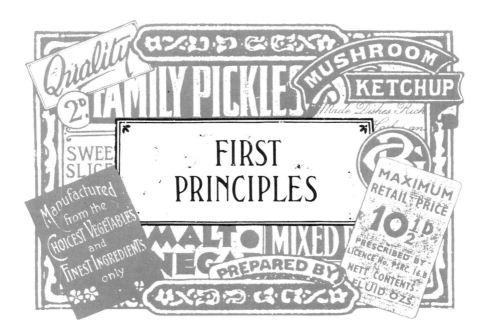

FIRST PRINCIPLES

Pickling is a way of preserving and transforming food. Often it relies on the effects of salt and vinegar, but not always. In this book we try to enlarge the subject, and to show there's much more to pickling than just onions in malt vinegar. It is a fact of life that food deteriorates and goes bad. Enzymes in the food itself cause the browning of cut surfaces and the change from pectin to pectic acid in over-ripe fruit. Yeasts, moulds and bacteria also attack food. Pickling is intended to keep the bacteria at bay. Originally it was a way of simply preserving seasonal crops through the year, but nowadays it can be used to create a whole larder full of new flavours and textures. New foods, in fact.

EQUIPMENT

One of the advantages of pickling is that it requires no special or expensive equipment. Most items are a standard part of any kitchen: sharp stainless steel knives which will not discolour fruit and vegetables; a large wooden chopping board; a colander; scales; a plastic or stainless steel funnel; a sieve; mixing bowls; stainless steel saucepans. It is important that you avoid copper, brass or iron pans which will react with the vinegar, discolour the pickles and produce unpleasant and potentially dangerous results.

Also you will need teaspoons and tablespoons for measuring and a set of wooden spoons for stirring and mixing. Don't use metal spoons when dealing with vinegar or brine.

An earthenware crock is very handy when pickling meat and fish, for salting cabbage and other vegetables and for making large quantities of any pickle.

The essential piece of equipment for making chutneys (as well as jams and marmalades) is a large stainless steel preserving pan, preferably with handles for safe and easy lifting.

Jars and containers are easy to come by. Unless you are making pickles for competition, there's no point in spending a lot of money on special jars. Collect empty jam jars, coffee jars, even re-cycled pickle jars, and ask your friends to let you have any they don't want. Pubs and restaurants are often a good source of large, wide-mouthed jars that are useful for pickled eggs and other big items. Try to use clear glass jars if possible, as well-made pickles are a treat for the eye.

Covering the jars is important. In the past there were all kinds of tricks, from writing paper soaked in brandy to melted paraffin wax or mutton fat. Avoid any cap or cover made of metal or with a metal lining: vinegar will cause this to corrode and taint the pickle. The best are plastic twist-on tops with a plastic, vinegar-proof lining. These are available in most good kitchen shops. If you have difficulty obtaining them locally write to the main manufacturer of these items: Lakeland Plastics, Alexandra Buildings, Station Precinct, Windermere, Cumbria LA23 1BQ (Tel: Windermere (096 62 2255). They also supply pickling and preserving accessories.

Chutneys can be covered with waxed paper discs and clear plastic, like jams, although they must be stored in a very dry place. Otherwise the twist-on plastic tops used for pickles are just as effective, and are more convenient once the jar has been opened.

WHAT CAN BE PICKLED?

The answer is virtually any kind of fruit, vegetable, and herb, as well as all sorts of meat, fish, poultry and game. During our travels we have seen everything from little Japanese aubergines coloured blue to Spanish caper berries that look like bald gooseberries on a stalk. We have uncovered recipes for pickling eels and pigeons and guinea fowl eggs. We have even tasted pickled crabs and grasshoppers, but we won't be supplying recipes for these esoteric delicacies!

Anyone who has a garden or allotment can tailor their cultivation to the needs of the kitchen, and that includes pickling. Most produce is grown for eating fresh, but it is easy to take advantage of gluts, and grow specifically with pickling in mind: pick your baby green tomatoes when they are the size of grapes, allow a few of your radishes to flower and go to seed so you can harvest the pods for pickling.

In the absence of home-grown produce, there is always the market. These days the range of fruit, vegetables and herbs is global. You don't need to go to Soho or Chinatown in London to buy rambutans or lemon grass: we have seen both on market stalls in Ludlow, Shropshire. Even on the east Suffolk coast it's now possible to buy all the ingredients for authentic Thai pickles as well as English stalwarts.

Whether you are growing and picking your own or buying from the market, there are a few golden rules. Above all, use the freshest produce you can lay your hands on. Pick from the garden and pickle within 24 hours. Don't be tempted to use pickling as an excuse for using up leftovers or stuff that would be better put on the compost heap. Second-rate ingredients produce second-rate pickles. Also try to follow the seasons, buy what is at its peak, and watch for bargains. Changes in cultivation and the fact that much produce is now imported mean that some vegetables, such as red cabbage, are now available right through the year, not just in the winter months.

Wild food can also be pickled. Our forebears took full advantage of a rich variety of herbs, nuts, berries and fungi—most of which are still to be found around the country. A glance through almost any recipe book of the seventeenth or eighteenth century would reveal pickles made from marsh samphire, alexander buds, ash keys, elder buds and much more. Armed with a copy of *Food for Free* by Richard Mabey (Collins/Fontana) you can track down many of these items and use them for exciting new pickles.

In Britain, we are still nervous about picking and eating wild fungi. Not so in Poland or Italy, where they are an essential part of the larder and are pickled as a matter of course. Scores of edible varieties grow in Britain, and they are worth getting to know. Obviously it is essential that you make use of a good identification guide. We would recommend *Mush-*

rooms and Other Fungi of Great Britain and Europe by Roger Phillips (Pan): it is clear, comprehensive and inspires confidence.

HERBS AND SPICES

Most pickles are brightened up with herbs and spices. They add bite, heat, fragrance and often colour as well. If possible use fresh or freshly picked herbs and don't be afraid to use them generously: a large sprig of fresh tarragon can transform a jar of pickled onions. Dried herbs do have their uses, especially in chutneys and other preserves that need to be cooked, but remember they taste stronger than their fresh counterparts, and can lose all flavour if they are old. With dried herbs, the rule is to buy small quantities regularly.

The same applies to spices. Always use whole spices, unless the recipe specifically states 'ground': they have a much higher concentration of aromatic oils, and consequently more flavour. Most supermarkets, good wholefood stores and grocers sell a wide range: there is a list at the back of the book (p. 153) giving names and addresses of useful specialist shops for some of the rarer items.

The quantities of herbs and spices given in the recipes are guidelines, rather than hard and fast rules. Don't be afraid to adapt, experiment, improvise and invent new flavours. And follow your own palate: if you don't like the flavour of cinnamon in pickled shallots, leave it out. In practice it will make very little difference to a pickle whether you use a 2 inch (5 cm) or 3 inch (7.5 cm) piece of fresh root ginger.

SALT

Salt is a preservative as well as a flavouring. It works in a complicated way by osmosis. Skin and cell membranes are semi-permeable: they allow liquid to pass through them, but the flow is always from the less concentrated to the more concentrated solution. When fruit, vegetables, meat or fish are put into salt or a strong solution of brine, liquid is rapidly drawn out of the tissues. At the same time, salt starts to flow much more slowly from the brine into tissues. This two-way traffic continues until the concentration of the brine and the cell fluids is the same. The salt has then 'struck through'. The combination of salt in the tissues and the lack of moisture inhibits the growth of micro-organisms, thus preserving the food.

Many pickle recipes include dry salting or steeping in brine as the first stage in the process, before the vinegar is added. Other pickles—particularly from Eastern Europe and Japan—are based purely on salt or brine. When making up a brine, use 2 oz (50 g) salt per 1 pint (600 ml) water. In most cases salting and brining can be done overnight: any longer and the salt flavour is likely to be too strong. Dry salting is best if you want a very crisp pickle.

There are four main types of salt: rock salt, which can be bought as unrefined crystals or, in a more refined state but without the addition of any chemicals, as 'block' or 'kitchen' salt; sea salt, which is produced by the evaporation of sea water using artificial heat; bay salt, which is similar but produced by natural evaporation using the heat of the sun; and the most common, table salt, which is highly refined and normally mixed with anti-caking agents such as magnesium carbonate and sodium hexacyano-ferrate II to give it free-running qualities.

If possible, avoid table salt for pickling: it is not as pure as the other types and has a dull flavour. The additional chemicals also slow down the rate at which the salt (sodium chloride) penetrates the tissues. Other kinds of salt may cost a little more, but they are worth it.

VINEGAR

Most pickles contain vinegar of some kind. Like salt it is a preservative, but it works rather differently. Bacteria and moulds grow best in a neutral or slightly alkaline solution. If the acidity is increased, bacterial growth is reduced. Vinegar contains acetic acid, usually about 5%, and this inhibits growth—especially if it is used with salt. Most commercially sold vinegar is required to have an acetic acid content of about 5%, and you can increase the concentration simply by boiling the vinegar for about 10 minutes before you use it.

There are several kinds of vinegar with different uses and qualities:
Malt vinegar:
The cheapest and most widely available vinegar, whose flavour has dominated English pickles for more than a century. As the name suggests it is made from malted barley, sometimes with cereal grain added. The starch in these raw materials is converted into sugars, which are fermented to give alcohol and finally acetic acid. Some brands are now produced without proper fermentation and many are also coloured with caramel. Malt vinegar does have a limited use, but the trend is definitely towards other vinegars with a finer, more subtle flavour. We would not recommend commercial ready-spiced malt vinegar: it is dull and predictable. Much better to make your own to suit your needs and the pickles you are making.

White (distilled) vinegar:

This is produced by distilling malt vinegar. It is colourless, and has a less pungent, sharper flavour. It is useful where the colour of the pickle is important, such as with red cabbages or French beans.

Spirit vinegar:

This is made by fermenting molasses. It is not normally sold in the shops, but is used for the commercial manufacture of pickles because it has a very high acetic acid content (usually 10–13%). The brutal acidity of many manufactured pickles is due to spirit vinegar.

Cider vinegar:

Time and again during our travels we have heard people recommending cider vinegar as the ideal pickling medium. This by-product of making cider has two great advantages: its mild, slightly fruity flavour and its quality. Some of the best brands, such as Aspall, are also produced from organically grown fruit.

Wine vinegar:

Chemically, this results from the fermentation of sugar in grapes to give alcohol, which is in turn fermented to form acetic acid. In practice, however, it is usually made directly from wine. The two most common are white-wine and red-wine vinegars, but there are more exclusive variations such as Champagne vinegar and Italian balsamic vinegar, which is made from the cooked and concentrated must of white grapes from Trebbiano, aged in wooden kegs for at least ten years. Although wine vinegars are expensive, the quality and flavour is excellent. In some recipes it is a good idea to mix wine vinegar with wine of the same colour to produce a slightly different effect.

Rice vinegar:

An import from the Far East, and in particular Japan, where it is called *su*. The pale yellow liquid has a very distinct, mild flavour. Although it is not used a great deal for Japanese pickles, it has been taken up by many enterprising cooks who are starting to mix the traditions of east and west. Rice vinegar is available from specialist Japanese food shops as well as a number of wholefood stores and oriental supermarkets.

ALTERNATIVES AND VARIATIONS

Flavoured and herb vinegars can also be used for pickles, but that is only half the story. In Japan, most everyday pickles use a mixture of rice bran, beer and salt; it is possible to pickle onions in Chinese soy or Japanese shoyu sauces; even *saké* (rice wine) is used occasionally. There's also a South American tradition of pickling fish in citrus fruit juice. In India many pickles use salt and mustard oil; in the Mediterranean, salt, wine vinegar and olive oil are common. Alcoholic liquors and spirits can also be used for pickling. Pickling is a vast subject, the possibilities are enormous.

TIPS FOR GOOD PICKLING

Pickling isn't an exact science, but it has ground rules. Follow these and you will have many more successes than failures.

1. Always use prime fresh ingredients. Discard any that are blemished, damaged or past their best.
2. Choose your vinegar wisely so that it enhances, rather than swamps, the flavour and appearance of the pickle.
3. Never use copper, brass or iron pans when making pickles.
4. In general, use dry-salting for pickles that are meant to be crisp, and brining for those that are soft.
5. Make up your own spiced vinegar using fresh whole spices. These can be boiled in the vinegar (either loose or in a muslin bag) for about 10 minutes. In some pickles it is essential to have the spices in the jar; in others they are simply used to flavour the vinegar and are strained off before bottling.
6. Jars should be cleaned in boiling water with soap, put upside down on a cloth to drain, then left to dry and warm at the bottom of a cool oven— gas mark 1 or 2, 275°–300°F (140°–150°C)—until needed. Don't dry the inside of the jars with a cloth as this may do more harm than good by spreading bacteria. The jars must be warm, not hot.
7. Always make sure the pickles are completely covered before sealing. If you want a very crisp pickle, leave the vinegar to get cold before adding it to the jar.
8. Cover the jar with a plastic twist-on top with a plastic seal inside. Avoid metal lids.
9. Make pickles in small batches. There's no point in putting all your onions in one huge jar because most of them will be far too old by the time you come to eat them. Anyway, you can always give a few little jars to friends as presents.
10. Label and date each jar when it is made.
11. Store pickles in a cool, dry place, preferably away from the light: light can make them dark and murky after a month or two.
12. Most important of all, realise pickles are not meant to keep indefinitely. As Carla Phillips of the Moorings Restaurant said to us: 'I'm

not making pickles for my grandchildren.' Some are past their best after one week, a few will survive well for six months, but in general a couple of months is the realistic shelf-life of most items.

Chutneys and relishes have their own rules in addition to the above.

1. Use stainless steel or aluminium pans and wooden spoons.
2. Even though the ingredients will be chopped and cooked to a pulp, they must be of good quality.
3. Light vinegar will make a light chutney, dark vinegar will make a dark chutney. Add the vinegar gradually and adjust the consistency as you cook.
4. The same applies to sugar. Choose it carefully. Always warm the sugar before adding it to the chutney, so it dissolves more quickly and doesn't caramelise at the bottom of the pan.
5. Use spices with imagination, but be sure to use a sufficient quantity. The blandness of many chutneys is due to a lack of enthusiasm for fresh spices. Again, you can taste and adjust the flavour towards the end of the cooking.
6. Cook the chutney without a lid, stirring well. To test when it is ready, draw a wooden spoon across the bottom of the pan: if it leaves a clean line, the chutney is ready to pot.
7. Use warm jars, not hot, otherwise the chutney will continue to cook and produce air bubbles on the inside of the jar. Put the chutney into jars while it is still hot.
8. Cover well with a twist-on top if possible. Label with the name and date of making.
9. Store the chutney in a cool, dry, dark place for at least two months, so the flavour can mellow and mature. Young chutneys are a shadow of the real thing.

THE ENGLISH TRADITION

'... the table would be laden with a big round of salt beef, a ham and bread and cheese and pickled onions, and with fare like that in front of you, a couple or three golden sovereigns in your money pouch to take home to mother, what else would a man want to do but sing? The songs came thick and fast, for the more they sang the more they drank—every song a drink was the rule—and the more they drank the more they sang ...'

(*A Song for Every Season* by Bob Copper, Heinemann, 1971)

That is how a famous Sussex farming and singing family remembered the celebrations in the pub after sheep shearing. Of course, there are other pickles, other memories. David Collison recalls his post-war childhood in the Lancashire town of Preston:

'My father was a prolific and expert pickler as well as an enthusiastic gardener—the two passions go hand in hand. Bottling of plums, apple-rings, rhubarb and tomatoes (the last truly revolting) was my mother's domain. The pickles were more fun to make and to eat: cucumber relish, pickled onions, horseradish and mustard sauce, and the inevitable green tomato chutney. In July there was another treat. After a hot—and frustrating—Tuesday or Friday selling yarn on the Manchester Cotton Exchange, my bowler-hatted pickling father would visit the street market by Manchester's Victoria Station. There, the first crop of green walnuts was waiting to be pounced on. They were borne home in triumph. Ten pounds of them were subjected to a mysterious regime which reminded me of school chemistry lessons, until eventually the jars of black, glistening spicy walnuts took their place on the pantry shelf. They were doled out ceremoniously like Maundy Money, but *never* stolen.'

Tradition really is the key to English pickling. And it stretches back hundreds of years, to a time when there were pickled alexander buds and samphire and damsons in the larders of great households and ordinary farm workers' dwellings. There was even an old 'cottage English' word for these specialities: they were called tracklements. Dorothy Hartley revived the word in her magnificent book *Food in England*, first published in 1954, and since then it has taken its rightful place in several dictionaries. Tracklements are more than garnishes or condiments, they include everything that accompanies a meal: both horseradish sauce *and* Yorkshire pudding are tracklements for roast beef.

There is a mood of revival too, and it is heart-warming to see pickles, chutneys, relishes and mustards being used in their true fashion by so many chefs and home cooks throughout the land. Here are game terrines with pickled damsons, roast quail served with Morello cherry relish, loin of pork stuffed with pickled quinces, smoked prawns accompanied by pickled asparagus. English pickles are back in the larder and back on the plate.

PICKLED ONIONS

Mention English pickles and most people think of pickled onions. The tried and tested idea of little onions in malt vinegar can work, provided you do not expect the pickle to keep for months on end without deteriorating. We reckon pickled onions for Christmas should not be started before the beginning of November: by the 24th December they will be coming to their peak.

After much experimenting with different ways of preparing the onions—soaking them in hot or cold water before peeling, dry-salting rather than brining them, dispensing with the brining altogether, pouring on the vinegar hot and cold—we decided the classic, well-tried method was still the most successful.

You can vary the spicing to suit your own palate. The mixture below produces punchy results.

Makes about 2 lb (1 kg)

2 lb (1 kg) pickling onions
2 oz (50 g) salt
1 pint (600 ml) malt vinegar
1 teaspoon (1×5 ml spoon) black peppercorns
1 teaspoon (1×5 ml spoon) coriander seeds
2 bay leaves
2 dried red chillies
1 oz (25 g) fresh root ginger, peeled and sliced

Peel the onions carefully with a sharp knife, removing only the minimum at the base and tip. Soak overnight in the salt mixed with 1 pint (600 ml) cold water. Next day, drain the onions and wash them in cold water to get rid of excess salt. Set aside to drain.

Put the vinegar in a pan with the peppercorns, coriander seeds, bay leaves, chillies and ginger and boil for 10 minutes. Set aside to get cold.

Pack the onions into cleaned, warmed jars, wiping each one with a cloth to get rid of the last traces of moisture. Pour on the cold vinegar. If you like a very strong flavour, include the whole spices in the pickle, otherwise strain them off. Make sure the onions are completely covered with vinegar. Seal the jars and keep for about 6 weeks before opening.

SWEET PICKLED ONIONS

Everyone has their own version of pickled onions. Margaret Borthwick, one-time National Demonstrator for the National Federation of Women's Institutes, does a sweet version, cleverly coloured with pieces of red and green peppers. Her trick to prevent the eyes from watering is to pour boiling water over the onions before peeling them.

Makes 2–3 lb (1–1.5 kg)

2–3 lb (1–1.5 kg) pickling onions, peeled
salt
6 oz (175 g) sugar
1½ pints (900 ml) white malt vinegar
1 teaspoon (1×5 ml spoon) mixed spice per jar
1 teaspoon (1×5 ml spoon) diced red and green peppers per jar
1 sprig fresh tarragon per jar

Put the onions into a large dish and sprinkle with plenty of salt, then leave overnight.

Boil the sugar and vinegar together until the sugar has dissolved, then set aside to cool. Rinse the onions well to remove all excess salt and wipe dry with a kitchen cloth. Pack the onions into jars adding mixed spice, peppers and a sprig of tarragon to each one. Cover with the cooled sugar and vinegar mixture. Cover and store for at least 2 months before using.

DAVID COLLISON'S PICKLED SHALLOTS WITH GINGER AND GARLIC

'I grow shallots each year—far more than is either sensible or necessary—then, to the horror of my gastronomic neighbours, I pickle them. Not my flask-shaped exhibition shallots, *Hâtive de Niort*, which are the pampered beauties of the local Horticultural Show, but Giant Red and Long Standing Yellow. Pickled shallots retain their crispness far longer than onions and have a milder flavour.' Peel the shallots with a very sharp stainless steel knife (some experts tell us that that the quality of a pickled shallot or onion is dictated by the peeling process).

Makes about 3 lb (1.5 kg)

1 inch (2.5 cm) stick cinnamon
12 allspice berries
12 cloves
1 heaped teaspoon (1×heaped 5 ml spoon) black peppercorns
1 inch (2.5 cm) cube fresh young root ginger, peeled and finely sliced
4 cloves garlic, finely sliced
4 dried red chillies
4 pints (2.25 litres) white malt vinegar
3 lb (1.5 kg) shallots, peeled
2 heaped tablespoons (2×heaped 15 ml spoons) salt

Put the spices and vinegar into a basin and place in a saucepan of water. Bring the water to the boil, but *not* the vinegar. Remove from the heat and allow the spiced vinegar to cool in the covered basin. After 4 hours strain the vinegar.

Place the shallots in a large bowl and sprinkle with salt. Mix, cover and leave for 12 hours.

Drain the shallots if you like a salty pickle. Otherwise rinse them thoroughly in cold water and leave to dry on a cloth. Pack 1 lb (450 g) or 2 lb (1 kg) jars with shallots and cover with the cold spiced vinegar. David adds 2 red chillies to each jar at this stage. Cover tightly and consume within 6 months.

PICKLED RED CABBAGE (1)

A hundred years ago, this pickle was described as 'perhaps the best article of its kind to be found anywhere, its excellency consisting in its flavour, its colour and its crispness'. That was the opinion of a certain Mr Robinson, a 'wholesale curer of comestibles' from Runcorn, who wrote *The Art and Mystery of Curing, Preserving and Potting* in 1864.

Pickled red cabbage has long been associated with traditional North Country food: it is the classic tracklement with Lancashire hot-pot, meat and potato pies and Lakeland 'tatie pot'. Its sharp, crisp flavour is the perfect foil for these heavy, bland dishes. Yet the sad truth is most cafés and restaurants now buy their red cabbage—and most other pickles—from the cash-and-carry or supermarket, even when they are resolutely baking pies and cakes in their own kitchens.

The secret of good red cabbage is not only in the light pickling, but in the shelf-life of the finished article. Within 2 weeks it is at its peak; after 4 weeks it is hardly worth eating. This is not a new idea: back in the eighteenth century, Mrs Elizabeth Raffald recommended pickled red cabbage would be 'fit for use in a day or two'. Quite right, too.

Makes about 1½ lb (750 g)

1 small red cabbage
2 tablespoons (2×15 ml spoons) salt
1 pint (600 ml) white vinegar
2 bay leaves (optional)
1 teaspoon (1×5 ml) black peppercorns (optional)

Choose a weighty, close-knit cabbage and cut off any rough outer leaves. Chop roughly so that there are all kinds of pieces—thin strips of leaf, chunks of stalk, which have different textures when pickled. Put into a large shallow dish, scatter salt over the cabbage and leave for 12 hours. Next day, wash the cabbage very thoroughly to get rid of all excess salt, then leave to drain in a sieve, shaking and patting with a cloth to get rid of the last traces of moisture.

Boil the vinegar with the bay leaves and peppercorns, if using, for 10 minutes. Leave to cool. Pack jars with the cabbage and pour over the cold vinegar, making sure that it is well covered. Seal and store for a couple of days before opening.

PICKLED RED CABBAGE (2)

An alternative recipe calling for demerara sugar and sliced onion. The sugar takes some of the acid bite out of the pickle and the onion makes its own savoury contribution. Once again, this pickle should be eaten very young, when it is still vivid red. As soon as the redness starts to dull, make lots of hot-pot and use it up. When it turns brown, banish it to the compost heap.

Makes about 1½ lb (750 g)

1 red cabbage, cored and roughly chopped
salt
1 small onion, sliced into rings
2 tablespoons (2×15 ml spoons) light demerara sugar
1¾ pints (1 litre) white malt vinegar
20 black peppercorns
4 bay leaves
dried red chillies (optional)

Put the cabbage into a large earthenware or glass dish and sprinkle salt between the layers. Leave overnight, by which time the cabbage will have turned a dull purple colour. Wash thoroughly under running water, then pat dry with a cloth.

Pack the cabbage into small jars, adding a few onion rings and a teaspoon of sugar here and there.

Heat the vinegar in a pan with the peppercorns and bay leaves. Allow to cool, then pour over the cabbage until it is covered. You can add a dried red chilli to each jar for extra heat and flavour. Cover and start to eat within 48 hours.

PICKLED ASPARAGUS

Opinions differ about the pickling of asparagus. In the great English country houses of the eighteenth and nineteenth centuries, huge prolific asparagus beds were essential, and cooks thought nothing of pickling two hundred stalks at a time. Nowadays it is a more precious crop, and its short season should be enjoyed to the full, when the stalks are fresh.

Even so a light pickle of asparagus in wine vinegar can be an occasional treat. The style of pickling hasn't changed much in two hundred years, as this recipe from *The Art of Cookery Made Plain and Easy* (1796 edition) by Hannah Glasse shows.

'Take the largest asparagus you can get, cut off the white ends, and wash the green ends in spring water, then put them in another clean water, and let them lie two or three hours in it: then have a large broad stew-pan full of spring water, with a good large handful of salt; set it on the fire, and when it boils put in the grass, not tied up, but loose, and not too many at a time, for fear you break the heads; just scald them, and no more, take them out with a broad skimmer, and lay them on a cloth to cool; then for your pickle take a gallon, or more according to your quantity of asparagus, of white wine vinegar, and one ounce of bay salt, boil it, and put your asparagus in your jar; to a gallon of pickle, two nutmegs, a quarter of an ounce of mace, the same of whole white pepper, and pour the pickle hot over them: cover them with a linen cloth, three or four times double, let them stand a week, and boil the pickle; let them stand a week longer, boil the pickle again, and pour it on hot as before; when they are cold, cover them close with a bladder and leather.'

Today's versions follow the same basic method, although the pickle isn't intended for long keeping. It is best eaten within a week of bottling. Victoria Stephenson, formerly of Bradfield House Restaurant in Suffolk, provides this recipe, which includes a couple of pieces of fresh angelica stalk from the garden for flavour and fragrance; alternatively you might try adding a few pieces of lemon peel to the pickle. The asparagus is a good addition to imaginative modern salads, and goes well with delicate cold smoked or fresh fish.

Makes about 2 lb (1 kg)

2 lb (1 kg) asparagus
10 fl oz (300 ml) dry white wine

10 fl oz (300 ml) white-wine vinegar
3 blades mace
2 teaspoons (2×5 ml spoons) white peppercorns
2 pieces fresh angelica stalk

Wash and trim the asparagus, cutting off the base ends and leaving about 6 inches (15 cm) of green stem. Put the stalks into a large saucepan of cold water so they are covered but not crammed together. Bring to the boil, remove from the heat and drain. Let the stalks dry on a cloth.

Heat the white wine, vinegar, mace and peppercorns in a separate pan for about 15 minutes. Leave to get cold. Pack the stalks of asparagus carefully into jars, tips upwards, then put in a couple of pieces of fresh angelica stalk. Strain the cold vinegar and pour over the asparagus until the tips are covered. Seal and store for a couple of days before using.

PICKLED CELERY

Choose the best autumn celery that appears in the shops during October and November. It has much more flavour and texture than the green cellophane-wrapped varieties. This pickle should be eaten young and it makes an interesting alternative to fresh celery, especially with hard English cheeses; it also goes well in winter salads. When the celery is finished, re-bottle the vinegar and keep it for use.

Makes about 2 lb (1 kg)

2 heads celery
1 pint (600 ml) cider vinegar
1 tablespoon (1×15 ml spoon) salt
1 oz (25 g) fresh root ginger, peeled and sliced
4 blades mace
1 red pepper, de-seeded and cut in thin strips

Cut the green tops off the celery, wash the white parts well and divide into stalks to fit your jars. Wipe them dry. Put the vinegar, salt, ginger and mace into a saucepan and boil for 10 minutes. Toss in the celery and the red pepper and boil for 2 minutes. Strain off the vinegar. Pack the celery into jars, keeping the stalks upright, and put strips of pepper among them. When the vinegar is cold, pour over the celery until completely covered. Seal and store in a dry place for 2 weeks before using.

PICKLED BEETROOT

This ranks with onions and red cabbage as the most popular pickle on the supermarket shelves. If you have a garden it's worth growing beetroot: you can pickle either whole baby beet or large specimens cut into pieces. Picklers of the past used to 'gimp them in the shape of wheels or flowers' or even turn them into 'various ornamental and grotesque figures'.

This recipe is for large beetroot. Serve simply with salads and cheese.

Makes about 1 lb (450 g)

1 lb (450 g) beetroot
salt
1 pint (600 ml) white vinegar or cider vinegar
1 teaspoon (1×5 ml spoon) black peppercorns
1 oz (25 g) fresh root ginger, peeled and sliced

Twist off the leaves of the beetroot, wash well and cook whole in a saucepan of salted water: they should be just undercooked rather than soft. Set aside to get cold, then peel and slice into pieces as you wish. Pack into cleaned, warmed jars.

Boil the vinegar with the peppercorns and ginger in a saucepan for 10 minutes. Strain off the spices, then set aside to cool. Pour the vinegar over the beetroot, making sure that it is completely covered. Seal and store in a cool, dark place. It is ready to eat as soon as it is made, but will keep for up to a month without deteriorating.

PICKLED JERUSALEM ARTICHOKES

An unusual crunchy pickle with a slightly oriental texture, not unlike water chestnuts, that can be added to a winter salad or used as an accompaniment for oily smoked sprats or smoked eel.

Makes about 1 lb (450 g)

1 lb (450 g) Jerusalem artichokes
1 teaspoon (1×5 ml spoon) salt
peel of 1 lemon, cut in ½ inch (1.5 cm) strips
2 bay leaves
10 fl oz (300 ml) white-wine vinegar

Peel the artichokes, so that you are left with neat rounded pieces which are easy to slice when served. Put into salted water, bring to the boil and blanch for no more than 5 minutes: they must not be cooked until they become soft.

Put the lemon peel and the bay leaves into the vinegar and boil for 5 minutes. Strain and allow the vinegar to cool. Set aside the lemon peel and bay leaves. Drain the artichokes well and pack into jars. Put strips of lemon peel and bay leaves among them and cover with the cooled vinegar. Seal and keep for at least 1 week before opening.

PICKLED KOHLRABI WITH SAFFRON

The colour and texture of this unusual pickle seem more Japanese than English. Florets of cauliflower can be pickled in similar fashion. It was devised by Tim Reeson, formerly of The Crown, Southwold, Suffolk, who, as a variation, sometimes includes pink peppercorns and dribbles a mixture of olive oil and walnut oil over the pickle to keep it moist and add more flavour.

Available from larger supermarkets or greengrocers, kohlrabi looks like a turnip with pale green leaves but is a member of the cabbage family.

Makes about 1 lb (450 g)

1 lb (450 g) kohlrabi, peeled and cut into pieces 2 inches (5 cm) long
1 pint (600 ml) white-wine vinegar
2 dried red chillies
1 stick cinnamon about 2 inches (5 cm) long
2 blades mace
1 teaspoon (1×5 ml spoon) cloves
1 teaspoon (1×5 ml spoon) coriander seeds
½ teaspoon (½×5 ml spoon) black peppercorns
pinch saffron

Blanch the kohlrabi in boiling water for 1 minute, then refresh under cold water. Drain well and set aside to cool.

Boil the vinegar with the remaining ingredients for 10 minutes, then set aside to cool. Strain off the whole spices. Pack the kohlrabi into a cleaned jar or a plastic tub and cover with the vinegar. Seal and leave for 1 week before serving. Do not keep more than 2 weeks.

MARROW MANGOES

Mangoes first appeared in England at the beginning of the eighteenth century, thanks to the traders of the East India Company. Cooks and housewives tried to imitate them by making use of cucumbers, lemons, peaches and melons. The idea was to hollow out the vegetable or fruit and stuff it with spices before pickling—just as housewives in India did with the real thing. Any genuine resemblance is debatable, but the results are amazingly potent.

This marrow recipe is a personal favourite. The beauty of the pickle is its unpredictable flavour. Each chunk is different, depending on the way the spices have been strewn over the marrow.

Makes 2–3 lb (1–1.5 kg)

1 marrow, weighing 2–3 lb (1–1.5 kg)
2 onions, chopped
1 teaspoon (1×5 ml spoon) grated fresh horseradish
2 teaspoons (2×5 ml spoons) white mustard seeds
1 oz (25 g) fresh root ginger, peeled and sliced
2 teaspoons (2×5 ml spoons) black peppercorns
1 pint (600 ml) malt vinegar
4 oz (100 g) light brown sugar

Peel the marrow, cut it in half lengthways, and scoop out the seeds. Put it in salted water to soak overnight.

Next day remove the marrow and allow to drain. Pack both halves with the onions, horseradish, mustard seeds, ginger and black peppercorns, scattering and spreading them at random. Tie the 2 halves together using 3 pieces of string along the length of the marrow, to prevent any of the filling seeping out. Put into a large stone jar or pot. Boil up the vinegar and pour it over the marrow. Cover with a cloth.

Next day drain off the vinegar, re-boil and pour over the marrow once again. Repeat each day for about 10 days, or until the marrow is dark and soft. Then take the marrow out, open it up and scoop out the spices. Slice the marrow into good chunks and pack into jars. Finally, boil up the vinegar with the sugar and pour it hot over the marrow. Leave to get cold, then cover and store for at least 2 months.

PICKLED COURGETTES

This is a world away from most recipes for pickled marrows and squashes. The combination of grainy whole mustard seed, honey and cider vinegar gives it the style of a condiment, with the vivid greenness and texture of the courgettes for contrast.

Makes about 1 lb (450 g)

1 lb (450 g) courgettes, thinly sliced
salt
1 teaspoon (1×5 ml spoon) turmeric
1 teaspoon (1×5 ml spoon) salt
2 teaspoons (2×5 ml spoons) white mustard seeds
2 tablespoons (2×15 ml spoons) clear honey
10 fl oz (300 ml) cider vinegar
2 onions, sliced into thin rings

Sprinkle the courgettes with salt and leave for 1 hour. Mix the turmeric, salt, mustard seeds, honey and vinegar in a pan, bring to the boil and simmer for 5 minutes. Leave to cool, skimming the surface, if necessary.

Drain the courgettes, wash well and pat dry. Pack into warmed, cleaned jars with the onion rings. Cover with the spiced vinegar. Seal well and store for 2–3 days before eating.

PICKLED FRENCH BEANS

This is a very quick, instant pickle that is not unlike a marinated vegetable salad. Tim Reeson formerly of The Crown, Southwold, serves something similar with chopped shallots and finely diced tomato flesh.

Makes about 1 lb (450 g)

1 lb (450 g) French beans, topped and tailed
1 teaspoon (1×5 ml spoon) salt
1 tablespoon (1×15 ml spoon) chopped fresh basil
5 fl oz (150 ml) sherry vinegar
1 tablespoon (1×15 ml spoon) walnut oil

Blanch the beans in boiling salted water for 3 minutes. Drain and refresh under cold water, then set aside to cool.

Transfer to a shallow dish, sprinkle with basil, cover with the sherry vinegar and mix well. Dribble a little walnut oil over the beans. Set aside in a cool place for a couple of hours before using. Remove the beans from the liquor and mix with other salad ingredients.

'AN EXCELLENT, AND NOT COMMON, PICKLE, CALLED SALADE'

A curious recipe which first appeared in *A New System of Domestic Cookery*, written by A Lady at the beginning of the nineteenth century. The Lady in question was later identified as Mrs E. Rundell. Surprisingly, soy sauce was already part of the English larder, a century and a half before the arrival of the first Chinese takeaways.

It is possible to make this pickle in a large-size coffee jar. We have found that the white wine adds little to the flavour. Instead, choose cider vinegar or white-wine vinegar for the best results.

'Fill a pint stone jar with equal quantities of onions, cucumbers, and sour apples, all cut into very thin slices, shaking in, as you go, a teaspoonful of salt, and three-parts of a tea-spoonful of Cayenne. Pour in a wine-glass of soy, the same of white wine, and fill up the jar with vinegar. It will be fit for use the same day.'

PICKLED ELDER SHOOTS

Arley Hall, a grand mansion only a few minutes' drive from the M6 in Cheshire, was the home of the Honourable Lady Elizabeth Warburton in the second half of the eighteenth century. Mrs Elizabeth Raffald was her cook and housekeeper, and in 1759 she decided to write down everything she knew. The result was *The Experienced English Housekeeper*, a book that has more than its share of marvellous English pickle recipes, from walnuts and kidney beans to barberries, samphire and radish pods.

Elder shoots were pickled too, as an imitation of newly discovered bamboo shoots—one of the edible treasures brought back to England by the men of the East India Company. Like many of Mrs Raffald's pickle recipes, this one calls for 'alegar' (vinegar made from sour ale).

'Gather your elder shoots when they are the thickness of a pipe-shank, put them into salt and water all night, then put them into stone jars in layers, and betwixt every layer strew a little mustard seed, and scraped horseradish, a few shalots, a little white beet root, and cauliflower pulled into small pieces, then pour boiling alegar upon it, and scald it three times, and it will be like piccalillo, or Indian pickle, tie a leather over it, and keep it in a dry place.'

A pickle in imitation of Indian bamboe:
'Take the young shoots of elder, about the beginning or middle of May, take the middle of the stalk, the top is not worth doing, peel off the out rind, and lay them in a strong brine of salt and beer one night, dry them in a cloth single, in the mean time make a pickle, of half gooseberry vinegar, long pepper, one ounce of sliced ginger, a few corns of Jamaica pepper, a little mace, boil it, and pour it hot upon the shoots, and stop the jar close up, and set it by the fire twenty-four hours, stirring it very often.'

PICKLED ALEXANDER BUDS WITH FENNEL

The Romans brought the alexander to Britain as a pot-herb. It thrived, became naturalised and was even cultivated like celery in nineteenth-century gardens. Today, its glossy green leaves are one of the first signs of spring along many roadsides, particularly on the east coast of England. Every part of this plant can be eaten and most parts can also be pickled. The young stems and tiny flower buds—like minuscule pale green cauli-flowers—are the best, and they can be pickled with fronds of young fresh fennel which starts to appear at the same time during April and May.

A few 2 inch (5 cm) pieces of young stem can be used if you are short of buds. Measure them by volume in a mug, as they weigh very little.

Makes about 1 pint (600 ml)

10 fl oz (300 ml) alexander buds
1 oz (25 g) salt
4 small fronds fresh fennel
1 oz (25 g) fresh root ginger, peeled and sliced
10 fl oz (300 ml) white-wine vinegar

Sort through the alexander buds, and use only those that are firm and tight. Watch for any signs of insect life! Blanch them (and any pieces of stem) in 1 pint (600 ml) boiling salted water for 10 seconds. Strain off the water, then refresh the buds under cold water and leave to drain.

Pack the buds into cleaned, sterilised jars, together with the fronds of fennel and slices of ginger. Pour over the cold vinegar and seal. This pickle can be eaten after 2–3 days, although it keeps surprisingly well for up to 3 months. Include it as part of an elaborate salad or as a tracklement for cold smoked fish.

PICKLED MARSH SAMPHIRE

Marsh samphire (*Salicornia europaea*) is a marvellous succulent plant that grows on saltmarshes round most British coasts, particularly in East Anglia. Until recently, the only way to get it was to pick the stuff yourself, but now it has become a fashionable vegetable and appears on market stalls and in fishmongers' shops—although much of the crop is imported from France.

To pickle or not to pickle, that is the question with samphire. The old Norfolk way was to pack the green stems into jars with vinegar and leave in the cooling bread ovens of the local bakery on Friday night. By Monday morning, they were perfectly pickled, it is claimed. Bernard and Carla Phillips, who run their restaurant right on the north Norfolk coast in Wells-next-the-Sea, disagree and would never dream of pickling samphire. On the other hand, Margaret Borthwick, ex-WI demonstrator, also living in Norfolk, showed us a jar she had made, which included little cubes of red pepper—her trademark as a pickler.

On balance, we reckon it is possible to pickle samphire successfully, provided it is done lightly and eaten quickly.

Makes 8 oz (225 g)

8 oz (225 g) marsh samphire
2 oz (50 g) salt
2 strips lemon peel
2 strips orange peel
10 fl oz (300 ml) white-wine vinegar or cider vinegar

Sort through the samphire and discard any mouldy or damaged pieces. Wash well and leave to drain. Make up a brine with the salt and 1 pint (600 ml) water, then bring to the boil. Plunge the samphire into it for 10 seconds to bring out its green colour. Remove and refresh under cold water and drain well.

Pack the samphire carefully into cleaned, warmed jars, keeping the stalks vertical if possible. Slip in the strips of lemon and orange peel for colour and flavour, then cover with the cold vinegar. The pickle is ready to eat the next day and is best consumed within a week. Try it with slices of cold lamb or a dish of fresh cockles and brown bread.

PICKLED NASTURTIUM SEEDS

'Nasturtian berries'—as they were called in the eighteenth century—were pickled as a peppery alternative to capers. They have a strange, pungent flavour which goes well with equally pungent fish such as skate, and can be used to brighten up indifferent salad leaves. Elizabeth Raffald again:

'Gather the nasturtian berries soon after the blossoms are gone off, put them in cold salt and water, change the water once a day for three days, make your pickle of white wine vinegar, mace, nutmeg sliced, pepper corns, salt, shallots, and horse-radish; it requires to be made pretty strong, as your pickle is not to be boiled; when you have drained them, put them into a jar, and pour the pickle over them.'

This recipe can be easily adapted for today's kitchens.

Makes 2 oz (50 g)

2 oz (50 g) nasturtium seeds (or as many as you can gather)
10 fl oz (300 ml) white-wine vinegar
1 teaspoon (1×5 ml spoon) salt
2 bay leaves
1 teaspoon (1×5 ml spoon) black peppercorns
2 blades mace

Pick the nasturtium seeds on a hot, dry day soon after the blossom has left the plant. Wash well, drain and put into a shallow dish. Leave in a cool oven (gas mark 1, 275°F (140°C)) to dry for about 10 minutes.

Put the vinegar, salt, bay leaves, peppercorns and mace in a saucepan. Bring to the boil and simmer for 10 minutes. Leave to cool. Pack the nasturtium seeds into jars with the bay leaves and spices. Pour over the cold vinegar and seal. Leave for 2–3 months before opening.

PICKLED RADISH PODS

Radish pods were highly rated as a vegetable for pickling by all the great recipe writers from Hannah Glasse to Mrs Beeton. They were pickled on their own and included as an essential part of mixed pickles and piccalilli. Like so many other interesting foods they seem to have gone out of fashion, which is a great pity because they have a unique pungent taste, not at all that of a cultivated vegetable.

To obtain radish pods, you need to grow radishes. All you have to do is leave one or two in the ground, let them grow and flower and eventually go to seed. Pick the seed pods once they start to form and before they become too bulbous.

Pickled radish pods are a useful alternative to chives and can be used like them in potato salad or with cream cheese.

Makes about 1 pint (600 ml)

10 fl oz (300 ml) radish pods
2 oz (50 g) salt
2 dried red chillies
10 fl oz (300 ml) white-wine vinegar

Pick the pods on a dry day, sort through them and discard any that are blemished or hard. Make up a brine with the salt and 1 pint (600 ml) water and plunge the pods into it while still hot. If they look bright green they are ready for pickling. If not, strain them off, re-boil the brine and repeat the process.

Strain off the brine and wash the pods under cold water to get rid of excess salt. Drain well and pack into clean, sterilised jars with the dried chillies. Heat up the vinegar and boil for 5 minutes, then cool. Pour it over the pods, seal and store for a couple of months. The pickle will keep until the winter.

PICKLED WILD MUSHROOMS

Bradfield House is a half-timbered seventeenth-century house in the village of Bradfield Combust—scene of a riot in the fourteenth century when the locals burnt down the hall. It is in deep, ancient west Suffolk, which is fertile fungus country. Victoria Stephenson used to gather all kinds of wild mushrooms from the conifer woods, including Slippery Jack (*Suillus luteus* or *Boletus luteus*). This makes a remarkable pickle, full of subtlety. Surprisingly it improves with age, and after six months it takes on an extraordinary sensual texture not unlike raw fish.

This is a pickle for cheese, and its flavour and texture are a good match for hard English farmhouse varieties. Soft, ripe French cheeses don't fare quite so well.

It is possible to make a reasonable imitation using ordinary cultivated mushrooms, or even oyster mushrooms, which are now 'farmed' extensively and available in most supermarkets. If, like Victoria Stephenson, you have white woodruff in your garden, this makes an unusual alternative to tarragon.

Makes about 2 lb (1 kg)

2 lb (1 kg) wild mushrooms, preferably Slippery Jack
2 teaspoons (2×5 ml spoons) salt
2 pints (1.2 litres) white-wine vinegar
2 bay leaves
6 cloves garlic, chopped
3 strips lemon peel
1 tablespoon (1×15 ml spoon) coriander seeds
1 teaspoon (1×5 ml spoon) black peppercorns
2 sprigs French tarragon

Clean the mushrooms with a damp cloth, but do not peel them. Put into a pan of boiling salted water for about 5 minutes. Drain thoroughly, then leave to dry and cool on a cloth.

Put the wine vinegar, bay leaves, garlic, lemon peel, coriander seeds and peppercorns into a saucepan. Bring to the boil and simmer for 10 minutes. Allow to cool. Pack the mushrooms into jars, and pour over the vinegar with the spices and other ingredients. Add a couple of sprigs of tarragon. Seal and store for at least 1 month before using.

PICKLED WALNUTS

Carole Evans, of The Roebuck, Brimfield, showed us her granny's hand-written recipe book, which contained barely legible instructions for making pickled walnuts. This is an adapted version of that recipe.

The problem with pickled walnuts is in getting a supply of young green nuts in June or early July. Huge numbers of walnut trees were cut down for French furniture makers in the nineteenth century. Many of the surviving trees are ancient and fruit unpredictably. There are also the grey squirrels, which can clear a complete tree overnight. Often you may have to procure imported French walnuts from a luxury greengrocer.

Makes about 1 lb (450 g)

1 lb (450 g) green ('wet') walnuts
2 oz (50 g) salt
1 teaspoon (1×5 ml spoon) allspice berries
1 teaspoon (1×5 ml spoon) black peppercorns
1 pint (600 ml) malt or white vinegar

Get the walnuts while they are green, before the shell has started to form. (The first bit of the shell appears opposite the stalk, about ¼ inch (0.5 cm) from the end.) Prick the nuts with a needle: there should be no obstruction. Make up a brine with the salt and 1 pint (600 ml) water and soak the nuts for about three days, then change the brine and soak for a further week. Drain well and spread the nuts out to dry—in the sun, if you are lucky, otherwise find some useful artificial heat. Turn the nuts so that they are well exposed and they will quickly turn black.

Boil the allspice and peppercorns with the vinegar for 10 minutes. Pack the walnuts into cleaned, warmed jars and pour the hot vinegar and spices over them. Seal and store for 1 month before using: the outside should be black, the inside still creamy and soft.

PICKLED EGGS

Fifteen years ago it was natural to walk into a pub and order a couple of home-made pickled eggs to go with your pint. Old stagers would eat them on their own, heavily peppered; new converts dropped them into packets of crisps and sometimes doused them with Worcestershire sauce. These days, the real thing is a rarity.

The Roebuck at Brimfield in Hereford & Worcester goes against the grain. Carole and John Evans run it as the village pub, with an admirable modern restaurant attached, and they have kept up the traditions of good home-made pickles: jars of their own chutney are sold across the bar; excellent pickled onions and cabbage decorate their bread and cheese lunches, and there's always a jar of pickled eggs made from the output of their free-range hens.

Carole Evans has a couple of useful tips about handling fresh eggs. First, she says, the way to shell them cleanly is to leave them in cold salted water for several hours after they have been boiled. Also, when they are being boiled it's worth stirring them round occasionally to keep the yolks in the centre of the eggs.

14 newly laid eggs
1 oz (25 g) fresh root ginger, peeled
1 tablespoon (1×15 ml spoon) white peppercorns
2 teaspoons (2×5 ml spoons) allspice berries
1½–2 pints (900 ml–1.2 litres) white vinegar
3 fresh red or green chillies

Put the eggs in cold salted water, bring to the boil and cook for 15 minutes, stirring occasionally. When the eggs are ready, drain them and leave in a bowl of cold salted water until ready to peel.

Tie the ginger, white peppercorns and allspice in a piece of muslin and boil in the vinegar for 5 minutes. Remove the spice bag and set aside the vinegar to cool.

Peel the eggs, pack into wide-mouthed jars and cover with the cold spiced vinegar. Add a chilli or two for colour and bite. Seal and store for a month before opening.

PICKLED QUAILS' EGGS WITH ROSEMARY FLOWERS

Fashionable, bite-sized quails' eggs are a novel challenge for picklers brought up on the harsh, dark brown pickled eggs of yesteryear. Victoria Stephenson flavours them with spices and garlic, and decorates them with rosemary flowers.

24 quails' eggs
2 pints (1.2 litres) white-wine vinegar
1 oz (25 g) fresh root ginger, peeled and chopped
3 cloves garlic, peeled
2 whole dried red chillies
1 teaspoon (1×5 ml spoon) cumin seeds
1 teaspoon (1×5 ml spoon) coriander seeds
a handful of rosemary flowers

Put the eggs into simmering water for about 3 minutes, drain and cover with cold water. Leave to cool, then shell carefully.

Put the vinegar into a large pan with the ginger, whole cloves of garlic, chillies, cumin seeds and coriander. Bring to the boil and simmer for about 10 minutes. Leave to cool. Pack the eggs into jars, top up with cold vinegar and spices, then float a handful of rosemary flowers on top. Seal and store. When serving, decorate with a sprig of fresh rosemary and some more flowers. The eggs are best eaten within 3 weeks.

PICKLED QUAILS' EGGS WITH BEETROOT

Tim Reeson, formerly chef at The Crown, Southwold, Suffolk, has a very different way of making pickled quails' eggs by mixing them with pieces of beetroot. This stains them pink and gives them a hint of sweetness: they look rather like plums in the jar. He uses Champagne vinegar as a flashy touch, but a standard white-wine vinegar will serve just as well. Tim presents these quails' eggs on a nest of watercress and alfalfa tossed with lemon and garlic dressing.

24 quails' eggs
3 oz (75 g) raw beetroot, peeled and diced
2 cloves garlic, peeled
2 dried red chillies
2 bay leaves
½ teaspoon (1×2.5 ml spoon) coriander seeds
½ teaspoon (1×2.5 ml spoon) black peppercorns
1 stick cinnamon, about 2 inches (5 cm) long
6 cloves
1 pint (600 ml) Champagne vinegar

Poach the quails' eggs in water for 3 minutes. Leave to cool in cold water, then shell. Put the beetroot into a pan with the garlic, chillies, bay leaves, coriander seeds, black peppercorns, cinnamon, cloves and vinegar. Bring to the boil and simmer for 10 minutes, then set aside to cool.

Pack the quails' eggs into a cleaned, sterilised jar with a wide neck. Pour in the vinegar, beetroot and spices, seal and store in a cool place. These eggs can be eaten after 2 days with the yolks still vivid yellow and whites paling out to pink at the edges, otherwise they should be consumed within 7 days.

PICKLED PLUMS

The success of this rich crimson pickle comes from bringing together two different types of plum—a tart, strong-tasting cooking plum like Blaisdon from the Forest of Dean, and a luscious dessert plum such as Victoria for its beautiful texture. By using the freezer you can take advantage of the different fruiting seasons of these two varieties and combine them when you want to make a pickle.

This recipe comes from Patricia Hegarty of Hope End Country House Hotel, near Ledbury, where plums are grown in abundance. She recommends serving the pickle with thin slices of good ham wrapped around curd or cream cheese mixed with fresh herbs.

Makes about 2 lb (1 kg)

1 lb (450 g) cooking plums
1 lb (450 g) dessert plums
8 oz (225 g) unrefined demerara sugar
10 fl oz (300 ml) cider vinegar
8 cloves
1 teaspoon (1×5 ml spoon) crushed cardamom seeds
sea salt and black pepper

Prick the smaller cooking plums with a needle to stop the skins from splitting. Cut the dessert plums in half lengthwise and remove the stones. (Both these jobs can be done very easily if the plums are still partially frozen.)

Dissolve the sugar in the vinegar in a heavy-based pan. Add the cloves and cardamom seeds, salt and pepper and the cooking plums. Soften the fruit over a gentle heat for about 5 minutes, then add the dessert plums and simmer for a further 10 minutes: the aim is to retain the shape of the fruit as much as possible. Lift out the fruit with a slotted spoon and pack into cleaned, sterilised jars. Reduce the pickling syrup and plum juice mixture by half, then pour hot over the fruit, making sure it is completely covered. Seal and store. It should keep well for up to 3 months.

PICKLED DAMSONS

It's not difficult to get hold of damsons. Many gardens have ancient trees that still bear a good crop of little dark fruit; some markets sell them in the early autumn and there are still trees to be found in the wild. The Lyth Valley, south of Windermere in Cumbria, is renowned for them.

Pickled damsons are the perfect accompaniment to good smoked ham as well as pheasant; they also go well with game pâtés and terrines.

Makes about 1 lb (450 g)

1 lb (450 g) damsons, stalks removed
8 oz (225 g) sugar
2 sticks cinnamon, each about 2 inches (5 cm) long
6 cloves
1 oz (25 g) fresh root ginger, peeled and sliced
10 fl oz (300 ml) white vinegar or cider vinegar

Pre-heat the oven to gas mark 1, 275°F (140°C).

Prick the damson skins with a needle to prevent them splitting, then put into an earthenware dish and sprinkle with sugar. Scatter the cinnamon, cloves and ginger over the fruit and cover with the vinegar. Put the dish at the bottom of a warm oven and leave to cook very slowly for about 20 minutes. Remove when the damsons begin to feel soft and the juice is running and set aside to cool.

When cold, strain the juice, boil it for 5 minutes and pour over the fruit. Repeat this straining and boiling every day for 1 week, then leave the damsons in the pickle for a further week, by which time the skins will be wrinkled and the juice will be the colour of vintage port.

Strain the damsons and pack into cleaned, warmed jars. Boil the juice once more and pour hot over the fruit. Seal well and store for 1 month before using: they improve with age.

PICKLED PRUNES

The old idea of soaking prunes in tea is quirky and good fun; it also gives the fruit a special flavour. This pickle benefits from long keeping, and is best after about 3 months on the shelf. Eat with cold ham.

Makes about 2 lb (1 kg)

2 lb (1 kg) prunes, pitted if preferred
juice and thinly peeled rind of 1 lemon
2 tea bags
1 pint (600 ml) malt vinegar
1 stick cinnamon
pinch freshly ground nutmeg
1 teaspoon (1×5 ml spoon) black peppercorns
2 tablespoons (2×15 ml spoons) brandy

Put the prunes in a large bowl with the lemon rind and juice. Brew the tea bags in a teapot, then pour over the prunes. Leave to stand for 24 hours. Strain the prunes and pack into cleaned, warmed jars.

Heat the vinegar in a pan with the cinnamon, nutmeg and peppercorns. Bring to the boil and simmer for 10 minutes. Strain through muslin, then pour over the prunes, making sure they are completely covered. Finally add the brandy, seal and store for at least 6 weeks before opening.

PICKLED GRAPES

For contrast, choose a mixture of black and white grapes. The idea is to create something delicate, slightly extravagant, slightly luxurious. Use wine vinegar to complete the effect.

Makes about 4 lb (2 kg)

4 lb (2 kg) grapes
1 pint (600 ml) white-wine vinegar
4 oz (100 g) sugar
1 tablespoon (1×15 ml spoon) cloves
1 tablespoon (1×15 ml spoon) finely chopped fresh root ginger
1 tablespoon (1×15 ml spoon) allspice berries
1 tablespoon (1×15 ml spoon) white peppercorns
1 tablespoon (1×15 ml spoon) salt

Cut only sound grapes from the bunches, discarding any that are blemished. Leave a tiny piece of stalk on each grape. Pack carefully into cleaned, warmed jars, shaking down well.

Put the vinegar, sugar, cloves, ginger, allspice, peppercorns and salt in a large pan, bring to the boil and simmer for 3 minutes. Leave to cool, then strain over the grapes, making sure they are completely covered. Seal and store. The pickle will keep well for a couple of months.

SPICED CHERRIES

Makes about 2 lb (1 kg)

2 lb (1 kg) cherries, stalks attached
1 bay leaf per jar
1 sprig fresh thyme per jar
10 fl oz (300 ml) white-wine vinegar
1 lb (450 g) sugar
2 sticks cinnamon, 2–3 inches (5–7.5 cm) long
2 blades mace
1 teaspoon (1×5 ml spoon) salt

Sort through the cherries and throw out any blemished fruit. Wash well and leave to drain. Pack into cleaned, warmed jars, with a bay leaf and a sprig of thyme in each. Put the vinegar and 5 fl oz (150 ml) water in a large pan, add the sugar and bring to the boil, stirring until dissolved. Add the cinnamon, mace and salt and simmer for 10 minutes. Strain the vinegar and leave to cool. Pour over the fruit, seal and store, keeping for up to 2 months.

MORELLO CHERRY RELISH

Dark black Morello cherries are at their peak for only a week or two in the summer. They can, however, be frozen successfully and used to make an excellent relish. Patricia Hegarty, of Hope End Country House Hotel, near Ledbury, gave us this recipe and recommends the relish with guinea fowl, turkey, goose or duck.

Makes about 1¼ lb (600 g)

4 oz (100 g) unrefined demerara sugar
6 fl oz (175 ml) cider vinegar

3 oz (75 g) onions or shallots, finely chopped
finely grated rind of 1 orange
½ teaspoon (1×2.5 ml spoon) ground cinnamon
½ teaspoon (1×2.5 ml spoon) ground allspice
1 lb (450 g) Morello cherries
sea salt and black pepper

Put the sugar and vinegar in a saucepan and cook over moderate heat for about 5 minutes, until the sugar has dissolved.

Blanch the onions or shallots in boiling water for 3 minutes, then strain well and add to the sweet-sour syrup. Mix in the orange zest, cinnamon, allspice and cherries. Simmer very gently so the cherries remain intact and the liquid gradually reduces and thickens. Season with salt and pepper, then pot the relish into warmed, sterilised jars. The relish can be used straightaway, but improves with keeping.

PICKLED REDCURRANTS

We have adapted this delectable recipe from *The Art & Mystery of Curing, Potting and Preserving* by A Wholesale Curer of Comestibles, 1864. It is neat, because it makes use of both bunches of fruit and single berries. It is best to pick the redcurrants yourself, so you have the right mix of fruit.

Makes about 8 oz (225 g)

1 lb (450 g) redcurrants (single berries)
8 oz (225 g) redcurrants (as bunches)
8 oz (225 g) sugar
1 oz (25 g) salt
2 bay leaves
1 pint (600 ml) white-wine vinegar

Pick redcurrants 'just before they have attained a perfect red colour'. Boil the single berries with the sugar, salt, bay leaves and vinegar for about 10 minutes, until the syrup is delicately coloured. Skim and set aside to cool. Strain through muslin and don't press the fruit as this will make the syrup cloudy. Boil up the syrup again, skimming, until it is perfectly clear.

Carefully arrange the whole bunches of fruit in cleaned, warmed jars and cover completely with hot syrup. Leave for 2 weeks before opening. The bunches can be removed and eaten like little bunches of grapes.

PICKLED QUINCES

Patricia and John Hegarty are champions of English food and produce an extraordinary range of fruit, vegetables and herbs at Hope End, their country house hotel near Ledbury. They grow quinces and have also resurrected many of the old varieties of perry pear, traditionally used to make the classic Herefordshire alternative to cider. Appropriately, their larder is lined with jars of quinces and pears preserved in perry. Patricia also produces pickled quinces and says they make a fine stuffing for rolled and roasted loin of pork or best end of neck of lamb flecked with bright green parsley and studded with a few cloves of garlic.

Makes about 2 lb (1 kg)

2 lb (1 kg) ripe quinces, peeled, quartered, cored and sliced
12 oz (350 g) unrefined demerara sugar
1 pint (600 ml) cider vinegar
finely grated rind of ½ lemon
6 cloves
2 teaspoons (2×5 ml spoons) allspice berries, crushed
¾ inch (2 cm) square piece fresh root ginger, peeled and halved
sea salt and black pepper

Keep the quinces in a bowl of salted water to prevent them discolouring.
    Dissolve the sugar in the vinegar in a heavy pan and add the lemon rind and the cloves, allspice and ginger tied in a muslin bag. Simmer for 5 minutes until you have a thin syrup. Strain the quinces, then add them to the pickle and cook slowly for about 10 minutes or until they have softened and the liquid has thickened. Remove the spice bag and season the pickle with sea salt and pepper. Pack tightly into cleaned sterilised jars and seal well. These quinces should keep through the winter but can be eaten after 2 weeks.

PICKLED LEMONS

This is our version of the pickle that delighted Elizabeth Raffald and other cooks in the eighteenth century. Eat it with hot spicy curries, cous-cous, pilaffs and other rice dishes. A similar pickle can be made using limes, but you should halve the quantity of salt.

4 lemons
3 tablespoons (3×15 ml spoons) salt
1 teaspoon (1×5 ml spoon) turmeric
1 teaspoon (1×5 ml spoon) cayenne pepper
10 fl oz (300 ml) cider vinegar

Wipe the lemons with a damp cloth and cut into chunks, removing the pips: do this on a plate to catch as much of the juice as possible. Pack the lemon pieces into a cleaned, sterilised jar.

Mix the salt, turmeric and cayenne with a little vinegar and add any excess lemon juice left after the chopping. Add this to the jar and top up with cold vinegar, making sure the lemons are completely covered. Seal the jar and give it a good shake. Leave in a warm place for at least 4 weeks, until the lemon skins have softened, shaking the jar occasionally. Store the pickle for at least 3 months before opening it.

SOUSED HERRING

Sousing is one of the classic English ways of pickling fish. It is special because the fish is actually cooked in the pickling liquid. Soused herrings should be eaten simply, perhaps garnished with fresh fennel and moistened with sour cream. If the fish have roes, enjoy these to the full—mash them up and spread on toast as a savoury accompaniment to the dish.

Sousing is equally good with fresh mackerel.

6 herring
1 onion, sliced
3 bay leaves
1 teaspoon (1×5 ml spoon) coriander seeds
2 dried red chillies
10 fl oz (300 ml) cider vinegar

Scale the fish, cut off the heads and draw out the guts, but keep them whole and leave any roes intact. Fit the herring into a shallow ovenproof dish and scatter the onions, bay leaves, coriander seeds and chillies around them. Pour over 10 fl oz (300 ml) water and the vinegar, cover the dish with foil and put into the bottom of a gas mark 1, 275°F (140°C) oven for about 1½ hours: the cooking must be slow and long. Let the dish cool down before you serve it. The fish will keep for 3 days.

LOBSTERS PICKLED IN CUCUMBER VINEGAR

This remarkable recipe is of purely historical interest, but it shows exactly what our pickling predecessors were prepared to attempt for their art and in the name of good food. It comes from *The Art and Mystery of Curing, Potting and Preserving* by A Wholesale Curer of Comestibles, 1864.

'In our hot summer months, and when lobsters are plentiful, it would be wise to save some that would come in opportunely for sauce and many dishes, when lobsters are scarce and high priced. Take fresh boiled lobsters, split them, take out the meat as whole as you can, and make a seasoning of

Mace, in fine powder 1 oz
Cayenne pepper ¼ oz
Nutmeg, in fine powder 1 oz
Table salt, in fine powder 6 oz

by well mixing them. Rub the meat well with this and equally so that no part is left undefended. Put the fish down in an earthen jar, and repeat the rubbing for a day or two. Pack it then in small jars and pour the following pickle over it, so that it may be covered to the thickness of an inch:

Best vinegar 1 pint
Chillies 1 oz
Cucumber vinegar ½ pint
Sal prunelle ¼ oz

and in similar proportions for each pint of vinegar used. Mind that the vinegar pickle covers well, and then put over all as much olive oil as will cover to the depth of half an inch. Tie wetted bladder over and leather upon that for safe keeping. It will be well recommended after a trial.'

SPICED BEEF

This was one of the great Victorian Christmas dishes. It was prepared and eaten by a generation with grander tastes than our own, yet it is still easy to make and is the perfect centrepiece for a seasonal cold supper with lots of pickles and tracklements.

A neat, round joint of silverside or topside is the best for this dish and you will need a piece weighing about 6 lb (2.75 kg) for the best results. Smaller pieces work quite well and larger ones are even better. Saltpetre

—available from chemists—is a necessary preservative when curing meat. It also produces an appetising pink colour: without it the meat would be murky grey after pickling. This is a modified version of Elizabeth David's recipe in *Spices, Salt and Aromatics in the English Kitchen* (Penguin, 1970).

6 lb (2.75 kg) joint of beef
3 oz (75 g) light brown sugar
1 oz (25 g) black peppercorns
1 oz (25 g) juniper berries
1 oz (25 g) allspice berries
4 oz (100 g) sea salt
¼ oz (10 g) saltpetre

Get the butcher to trim and tie the meat into a neat round. Rub it all over with sugar and put into a large pot with a lid for 2 days. Leave in a cool place, turning and occasionally rubbing the meat with the sticky liquor.

Crush the peppercorns, juniper and allspice with a pestle and mortar and mix with the salt and saltpetre. Rub this mixture well into the meat and leave in the pot for a further 9 days. During this time you must tend the beef every day, turning it and rubbing the pickle well into the flesh.

When the pickling is complete, remove the beef and rub off any excess spices adhering to the surface. Do not rinse it. Wrap the meat in cooking foil (the Victorians used suet) and put into a large ovenproof pot. Add about 10 fl oz (300 ml) water to the pot and cover the top with a double layer of foil, then fit the lid on tightly.

Pre-heat the oven to gas mark 1, 275°F (140°C). Bake the meat slowly, allowing 45 minutes per 1 lb (450 g). When the meat is cooked, remove the pot and set aside until quite cold: this will take several hours. Unwrap the meat, drain off any excess liquid and place on a board. Cover with a piece of foil and place a heavy weight on it, then leave for 24 hours.

Carve the meat into thin slices and serve with anything from good mustard to pickled kumquats. It will keep well in the fridge if wrapped in foil.

PICKLED BELLY PORK

'You can't get many pimples on a pound of pickled pork', runs the old music hall song by Ernie May. Follow this recipe to the letter and you should have none at all!

Pickling, or sousing, pork went hand in hand with pig killing and for centuries it was one of the staple meats in every country household. Autumn was the time for killing the pig. The sides and the hams were salted down to provide supplies of bacon through the winter. Most of the other bits—trotters, ears, cheeks and so on—were put into a tub of brine and soused. Although brine was the most common 'sousing drink', some better-off households also used verjuice and wine or ale with spices. The pork was ready for Christmas, when it was part of good 'husbandly fare':

> 'Good bread and good drinke, a good fier in the hall,
> Brawn, pudding, and souse, and good mustarde withal.'
> (Thomas Tusser, 1571)

Today's pickled pork is very different, but it is one of the easiest and most successful kinds of pickled meat you can produce at home. Any cut can be used, but belly is one of the best bets. Do the pickling in an earthenware crock, a plastic bucket or a pedal bin. It is important to clean this thoroughly with hot water and washing soda before starting.

3 lb (1.5 kg) piece belly pork
12 oz (350 g) sea salt
1 oz (25 g) saltpetre
1 teaspoon (1×5 ml spoon) black peppercorns
1 teaspoon (1×5 ml spoon) allspice berries
4 oz (100 g) light brown sugar (optional)

Clean all your equipment thoroughly before you start—including wooden spoons, tongs for turning the meat and so on. Make the brine by heating the salt and saltpetre with 4 pints (2.25 litres) water in a large pan. Add the peppercorns and allspice tied in a muslin bag: if you want a sweet-pickled pork, also add the sugar to the brine. Boil for 10 minutes, skimming off any froth that forms, then let the brine cool down and strain it through muslin into the pickling crock or bucket.

When the brine is completely cold, add the meat and keep it submerged with a piece of cleaned and boiled wood. Stir the brine occasionally with a wooden spoon and turn the meat using cleaned tongs.

The meat will be ready after 3 days in brine: larger pieces will take longer, but the pickling time depends more on the thickness of the meat than its actual weight.

Remove the meat with tongs and drain, then cook it. If you want a very mild flavour, soak the meat in cold water for 30 minutes before cooking. Excellent served with broad beans or a purée of split peas.

SPICED PICKLED CHICKEN

Tim Reeson of The Crown, Southwold, discovered this by chance. The story goes that a couple of chicken breasts accidentally found their way into the pickling mixture he uses for beef. They lay unnoticed for a few days at the bottom of the tub, before coming to light. After some experimenting and refinement, the result was this recipe.

Eat the chicken cold, cut into strips and served with mayonnaise flavoured with whole-grain mustard.

4 chicken breasts, skinned
4 dried red chillies
2 bay leaves
1 stick cinnamon, about 2 inches (5 cm) long
1 oz (25 g) fresh root ginger, peeled
1 teaspoon (1×5 ml spoon) cloves
1 teaspoon (1×5 ml spoon) coriander seeds
½ teaspoon (½×5 ml spoon) black peppercorns
pinch ground mace
pinch salt
10 fl oz (300 ml) white-wine vinegar

Arrange the chicken in a shallow dish so the pieces do not overlap.

Put the remaining ingredients in a large pan and bring to the boil, then simmer 5 minutes. Remove from the heat and leave to cool. Pour over the chicken and leave to marinate 3 days.

Transfer everything to a large saucepan and slowly bring to the boil, then immediately remove from the heat. Leave the chicken to cool in the vinegar mixture. Remove when cold, wrap in cling film and store in the fridge where it will keep for up to a week.

PICKLED PIGEONS (1)

The tradition of pickling all kinds of game birds stretches right across the globe, and we have discovered recipes from countries as far apart as India and Argentina. This extraordinary eighteenth-century English recipe is not only complex and intriguing, but is exactly in tune with the vivid style of many of today's young English chefs. The recipe comes from *Five Hundred New Receipts in Cookery* by John Middleton, revised and recommended by Henry Howard, 1734.

'Take twelve pigeons, bone half of them, and take off the flesh of the other half, and beat it fine as sausagemeat; mix it with salt, pepper, spices and herbs, a little marrow, some lemon peel, three anchovies, and the yolks of three or four hard eggs, stuff your pigeons that you boned full of it; the Herbs must be Sorrel and Spinage, young beets, thyme, marjoram and savory; make your pickle of water and white wine, a bay leaf or two and a little salt; boil the bones in the pickle, and when they are enough take them out, and let them to be cold; then put your pigeons in to keep.'

We haven't attempted this recipe, but we offer it as a challenge to any enterprising chef with a feel for real English food.

PICKLED PIGEONS (2)

Slightly less daunting is this recipe, which we have adapted from *A New System of Domestic Cookery* by A Lady, 1829.

6 pigeon breasts
1 teaspooon (1×5 ml spoon) salt
1 teaspoon (1×5 ml spoon) ground allspice
10 fl oz (300 ml) dry white wine
10 fl oz (300 ml) white-wine vinegar
3 bay leaves
2 teaspooons (2×5 ml spoons) allspice berries
1 teaspoon (1×5 ml spoon) white peppercorns
1 oz (25 g) fresh root ginger, peeled and sliced
½ whole nutmeg

Get the butcher to trim and prepare the pigeon breasts, removing skin and any fat. Mix the salt and allspice together and season the meat with it.

Plunge the breasts into a pan of boiling water for 1 minute, then take them out and dry well.

Put the wine, vinegar, bay leaves, allspice, peppercorns, ginger and nutmeg into a separate pan, bring to the boil and simmer 5 minutes. Add the pigeons, bring to the boil again and simmer a further 5 minutes. Remove from the heat and leave the pigeons to cool in the liquid.

When cold, take them out and serve sliced with salads and fruity relishes. They will keep for 3 or 4 days.

GREEN TOMATO CHUTNEY (1)

This chutney is an economical way of using up green tomatoes—either unripened fruit from your garden, or from shops in September and October. There are many recipes, some using sugar, others treacle; some with curry spices, others with just cayenne pepper and mustard. Some versions are pulpy, others have a much coarser, more chunky consistency.

Makes about 4 lb (2 kg)

2 lb (1 kg) green tomatoes
8 oz (225 g) onions, chopped
8 oz (225 g) cooking apples, peeled, cored and chopped
10 fl oz (300 ml) cider vinegar
4 oz (100 g) sultanas
1 teaspoon (1×5 ml spoon) salt
½ teaspoon (1×2.5 ml spoon) cayenne pepper
½ teaspoon (1×2.5 ml spoon) dry mustard
8 oz (225 g) light brown sugar

Skin the tomatoes by blanching in hot water for 30 seconds. Chop the flesh and put into a preserving pan with the onions and apples. Add about half the vinegar and cook gently until the fruit and vegetables are soft, stirring frequently. Add the remaining vinegar with the sultanas, salt, cayenne pepper, dry mustard and sugar and continue to cook slowly about 15 minutes until the chutney starts to thicken. Pot while still slightly runny, and seal the jars. It will keep for at least 3 months.

GREEN TOMATO CHUTNEY (2)

Makes about 3 lb (1.5 kg)

2 lb (1 kg) green tomatoes, roughly sliced
1 lb (450 g) onions, sliced
salt
2 teaspoons (2×5 ml spoons) plain flour
2 teaspoons (2×5 ml spoons) dry mustard
1 teaspoon (1×5 ml spoon) curry powder
1 teaspoon (1×5 ml spoon) turmeric
½ teaspoon (1×2.5 ml spoon) cayenne pepper
½ teaspoon (1×2.5 ml spoon) ground mixed spice
1 pint (600 ml) cider vinegar
2 tablespoons (2×15 ml spoons) treacle

Put the tomatoes and onions in a bowl, sprinkle with salt and leave for 12 hours.

Blend the flour, dry mustard, curry powder, turmeric, cayenne pepper and mixed spice with a little of the vinegar to make a smooth paste. Add to the remaining vinegar and mix in a large pan with the treacle. Strain the tomatoes and onions, wash well to remove excess salt and pat dry. Add to the pan and simmer for up to 45 minutes. When the chutney has thickened, leave it to cool before packing into jars. It will keep for at least 3 months.

GREEN TOMATO CHUTNEY (3)

This recipe is part of Collison family mythology and is said to have originated in Australia. It is a chutney with a difference, in that the thickening agent is semolina, giving the chutney an excellent texture.

Makes about 4 lb (1.75 kg)

4 lb (1.75 kg) green tomatoes, chopped
12 oz (350 g) cooking apples, peeled, cored and chopped
2 lb (1 kg) light demerara sugar
12 shallots or small onions, chopped
3 oz (75 g) salt
1 teaspoon (1×5 ml spoon) cayenne pepper

2 oz (50 g) semolina
2 pints (1.2 litres) malt vinegar

Put the tomatoes and apples into a preserving pan with the sugar and
slowly bring to the boil, stirring well. Cover and simmer over a very low
heat for 1½ hours, then add the shallots, salt and cayenne pepper.

Blend the semolina with 1 tablespoon (1×15 ml spoon) of the vinegar
and stir into the mixture. Add the remaining vinegar, bring to the boil,
then reduce the heat and simmer for a further 30 minutes, stirring from
time to time. Pack into warmed jars, cover and seal in the usual way and
store for a couple of months before opening.

RED TOMATO CHUTNEY

One of Davilia David's friends provided us with the recipe for this popular English chutney. As well as perking up cold meats and cheeses, it goes
brilliantly with bacon and eggs, and can add a new twist to tomato-based
sauces.

Makes about 5 lb (2.25 kg)

3 lb (1.5 kg) red tomatoes, peeled and roughly chopped
2 lb (1 kg) cooking apples, peeled and chopped
8 oz (225 g) onions, chopped
1 oz (25 g) pickling spice
1 oz (25 g) dry mustard
1 oz (25 g) salt
10 fl oz (300 ml) cider vinegar
8 oz (225 g) sultanas
12 oz (350 g) light brown sugar

Place the tomatoes in a large pan with the apples and onions. Wrap the
pickling spice in a muslin bag, add to the mixture and begin to simmer
gently, pouring in a little water if it begins to stick. Blend the mustard and
salt with a little vinegar and stir into the mixture. When the ingredients
have softened, add the sultanas, sugar and remaining vinegar. Continue
to simmer, stirring all the time, until the chutney is thick and smooth.
Pack into warm jars, cover and store for 2 months before opening.

SWEET GREEN PICKLE

The ancient style of the mixed vegetable pickle has been adapted over the years. This recipe from Sue Elston, who sells an excellent range of home-made pickles in her provisions shop in Burnham Market, has more in common with the originals than many present-day versions of so-called piccalilli. It is a pickle to be made in bulk and it should follow the seasons: at some times of the year it is much 'greener' than others. Adapt the recipe to your needs but be sure to use vegetables that are plentiful and in their prime.

Makes about 12 lb (5.5 kg)

4 red peppers, de-seeded and chopped
2 large cucumbers, sliced
3 green peppers, de-seeded and chopped
1 cauliflower, broken into florets
2 lb (1 kg) onions, chopped
6 lb (2.75 kg) green tomatoes, roughly chopped
1 lb (450 g) courgettes, sliced
3 oz (75 g) salt
1¼ pints (750 ml) cider vinegar
2 teaspoons (2×5 ml spoons) turmeric
1 oz (25 g) black mustard seeds
2 teaspoons (2×5 ml spoons) celery seeds
2 oz (50 g) plain flour
2 lb (1 kg) sugar

Place the vegetables in a large bowl, sprinkle with salt and cover with water. Stir well, cover and leave overnight. Next day, drain off the brine and transfer the vegetables to another pan with 10 fl oz (300 ml) vinegar. Add 8 fl oz (250 ml) water and bring to the boil, then drain immediately: do not allow the vegetables to cook.

Meanwhile make the sauce—or 'gloop' as it is called in north Norfolk. Put the remaining vinegar in a separate pan, stir in the turmeric, the mustard and celery seeds and add the flour, moistened and blended with a little vinegar to make it smooth. Warm the pan and add the sugar, stirring well until dissolved, then continue simmering until the mixture has thickened, stirring regularly. When the sauce is ready, mix with the vegetables. Fill into warmed jars, seal and keep for 1 month before opening.

PICCALILLI

There are many versions of this classic mixed pickle, and you can vary the types and quantities of vegetables depending on what is at hand. Davilia is holding a jar of piccalilli on the jacket of this book.

Makes about 1½ lb (750 g)

8 oz (225 g) cauliflower, broken into small florets
8 oz (225 g) small courgettes, sliced into rings
4 oz (100 g) green tomatoes, chopped
4 oz (100 g) baby onions, peeled and left whole
1 red pepper, de-seeded and cut into cubes
1 cucumber, cut into cubes
2 tablespoons (2×15 ml spoons) salt
1 tablespoon (1×15 ml spoon) dry mustard
2 teaspoons (2×5 ml spoons) turmeric
2 teaspoons (2×5 ml spoons) ground ginger
1 tablespoon (1×15 ml spoon) plain flour
1 pint (600 ml) white or cider vinegar
½ teaspoon (1×2.5 ml spoon) celery seeds
2 oz (50 g) sugar (optional)

Put all the vegetables into a large bowl and sprinkle with salt and leave overnight. (Dry salting is better than brining because it helps the vegetables to retain their crispness.) Next day, wash the vegetables free of excess salt and drain well.

Mix the mustard, turmeric and ginger with the flour and a little vinegar to make a smooth paste. Put into a saucepan with the remaining vinegar, celery seeds, and sugar (if you want a sweet pickle). Bring to the boil, then simmer for 15 minutes, stirring well until the sauce has thickened. Pack the vegetables into cleaned, warmed jars and cover with the hot mustard sauce, agitating the jars slightly so there aren't any air pockets. Seal the jars and store for 1 month before opening. This pickle should keep well for up to 3 months before it starts to discolour and dry out.

AUNTIE NITA'S APPLE CHUTNEY

The ladies of the Mere and Over Tabley WI made this chutney as part of their entry for the 1988 Cheshire Show. For the second year running they won first prize, this time with a score of 19½ out of 20.

Makes about 4 lb (2 kg)

2 lb (1 kg) cooking apples, peeled, cored and finely chopped or minced
1 lb (450 g) onions, finely chopped or minced
1 pint (600 ml) malt vinegar
1 lb (450 g) sultanas
1 oz (25 g) whole pickling spice
1 teaspoon (1×5 ml spoon) ground allspice
1 teaspoon (1×5 ml spoon) ground ginger
½ teaspoon (1× 2.5 ml spoon) salt
1 lb (450 g) soft light brown sugar

Put the apples and onions into a preserving pan with a little vinegar and simmer until soft. Add the sultanas, pickling spice (tied in a muslin bag and bruised), allspice, ginger and salt, together with the remaining vinegar and simmer gently until the apples and onions have reduced to a pulp. Warm the sugar in a very cool oven (gas mark 1, 275°F (140°C)), then stir it into the mixture, stirring until the chutney has thickened and a wooden spoon can be drawn cleanly across the bottom of the pan. Pour into warmed jars, seal and store for at least 3 months before eating.

UNCOOKED APPLE AND PEAR CHUTNEY

Australians—and Cockneys—call this Stairs Pickle, for obvious reasons. It is unusual because it is like an uncooked chutney. Also, it doesn't contain any added sugar, which might be a plus for weight-watchers.

Makes about 3 lb (1.5 kg)

1 lb (450 g) cooking apples, peeled, cored and finely chopped or grated
1 lb (450 g) firm pears, peeled, cored and finely chopped or grated
1 oz (25 g) fresh root ginger, peeled and finely chopped
2 cloves garlic, finely chopped
1½ lb (750 g) raisins

1 teaspoon (1×5 ml spoon) cayenne pepper
2 teaspoons (2×5 ml spoons) salt
1½ pints (900 ml) cider vinegar

Mix the apples and pears in a bowl with the ginger and garlic. Add the raisins, cayenne pepper, salt and vinegar. Stir thoroughly and leave in a cool place for 3 days, stirring from time to time. Pack into clean jars and seal well. The chutney will keep for about 1 month.

APRICOT AND ORANGE CHUTNEY

A recipe from Margaret Borthwick, who says it goes well with cold ham and mild curries. Dried apricots have a stronger flavour than fresh ones.

Makes about 3 lb (1.5 kg)

1 lb (450 g) dried apricots, soaked overnight
4 oranges
2 onions, finely chopped
3 cloves garlic, crushed
8 oz (225 g) sultanas
2 tablespoons (2×15 ml spoons) allspice berries
2 tablespoons (2×15 ml spoons) coriander seeds
1 tablespoon (1×15 ml spoon) white mustard seeds
2 teaspoons (2×5 ml spoons) ground ginger
1 tablespoon (1×15 ml spoon) salt
1½ pints (900 ml) white malt vinegar
1 lb (450 g) sugar

Drain the apricots and put into a large preserving pan. Take off the zest and fine peel of the oranges and add to the apricots. Roughly chop the orange flesh, making sure there is no bitter pith with it, then add to the pan with the onions, garlic and sultanas. Put the whole spices into a muslin bag, tie up and roughly crush. Add to the pan.

Stir in the ground ginger and salt. Add about 1 pint (600 ml) vinegar and blend well. Warm the sugar and stir into the pan. Stir regularly to avoid sticking and thin with the remaining vinegar if desired. Continue to cook for about 1 hour until the chutney is quite smooth and pulpy. Pack into warm jars, seal and store for a couple of months before using.

APRICOT AND DATE CHUTNEY

This chutney was devised by Sybil Norcott and her colleagues from the Dunham Massey Women's Institute as part of their entry in the 1988 Cheshire Show. Their theme was The Return of the Cheshire Regiment and the chutney was intended to have a spicy flavour with echoes of colonial India.

Makes about 2 lb (1 kg)

1 lb (450 g) dried apricots, soaked overnight and drained
1 teaspoon (1×5 ml spoon) white mustard seeds
1 teaspoon (1×5 ml spoon) whole pickling spice
8 oz (225 g) onion, chopped
8 oz (225 g) stoned dates, chopped
1 teaspoon (1×5 ml spoon) turmeric
1 teaspoon (1×5 ml spoon) curry powder
finely grated rind and juice of 1 orange
salt
1 pint (600 ml) white malt vinegar
1 lb (450 g) sugar
pinch ground mixed spice, or to taste

Roughly chop the apricots. Put the mustard seeds and pickling spice into a piece of muslin and tie up with a long piece of string. Crush the spices with something heavy and tie the bag to the handle of the preserving pan.

Put the apricots, onions and dates into the pan, with the turmeric, curry powder, orange rind and juice, and a pinch of salt. Add half the vinegar and simmer gently until the apricots are cooked, adding a little more vinegar if the mixture starts drying out.

Pre-heat the oven to gas mark 1, 275°F (140°C) and warm the sugar for 10–15 minutes. Also warm your clean jam jars ready for packing.

Remove the preserving pan from the heat, add the warmed sugar and stir until dissolved, then return to the heat and continue to cook. Reduce the heat and simmer until the chutney has a smooth consistency: test by drawing a spoon across the bottom of the pan. Taste the chutney and add a pinch of mixed spice if necessary. Pot in warmed jars and cover while hot. Store for at least 3 months in a dark place before opening.

PEACH CHUTNEY

Makes about 3 lb (1.5 kg)

2 lb (1 kg) yellow-fleshed peaches, peeled, stoned and roughly chopped
8 oz (225 g) cooking apples, peeled, cored and chopped
8 oz (225 g) onions, thinly sliced
8 oz (225 g) seedless raisins, finely chopped
12 oz (350 g) light brown sugar
2 oz (50 g) preserved ginger, finely chopped
2 cloves garlic, crushed
2 teaspoons (2×5 ml spoons) salt
1 teaspoon (1×5 ml spoon) cayenne pepper
15 fl oz (450 ml) white-wine vinegar

Mix the peaches, apples, onions, raisins, sugar, ginger, garlic, salt and cayenne pepper together in a large pan. Add the vinegar and stir over a low heat until the sugar has dissolved, then cook very slowly for about 1½ hours, stirring regularly. When the chutney has a smooth, thick consistency, remove from the heat and allow to cool slightly before packing into jars. Cover and seal when cool. It will keep for up to 6 months.

LEMON AND MUSTARD SEED CHUTNEY

Sue Elston's admirable provisions shop in Burnham Market is noted for its pickles and chutneys, many of which are made by local ladies.

Makes about 2 lb (1 kg)

4 large lemons, well wiped and finely chopped with pips removed
8 oz (225 g) onions, finely chopped
1 oz (25 g) salt
1 oz (25 g) white mustard seeds
1 teaspoon (1×5 ml spoon) ground ginger
1 teaspoon (1×5 ml spoon) cayenne pepper
4 oz (100 g) sultanas
1 lb (450 g) sugar
1 pint (600 ml) cider vinegar

Mix the lemons, onions and salt together and leave overnight.

Next day put the contents of the bowl into a preserving pan and simmer the ingredients until soft, adding a little water if necessary. Stir in the
mustard seeds, ginger and cayenne pepper, sultanas, sugar and vinegar.
Mix well and continue to cook for about 30 minutes until thick. Spoon or
pour into warm jars, seal and store for a couple of months before using.

WHOLE-GRAIN MUSTARD

Mustard is a big subject. It is one of the great tracklements and, as such,
deserves a mention in any book about pickles. Making your own mustard
can be great fun, although we would recommend that you begin by experimenting with small quantities and different flavourings before em-
barking on anything too substantial. You can start, like William Tullberg
of Wiltshire Tracklements, with a bag of seed and a coffee grinder.

It isn't possible to give precise quantities, but we have outlined the general principles and method. The rest is up to you.

Buy your mustard seeds from a seed merchant, wholefood shop or delicatessen that sells in bulk.

Use a mixture of black (or brown) and white seeds. Try equal amounts
to begin with, but vary the proportions to suit your taste and the style of
mustard you want. Grind the seed with a coffee grinder for finely ground
mustard or pestle and mortar for coarser varieties—or a combination of
both. Put it into a big stoneware or glass jar and moisten with a little water.

Add sufficient cider vinegar or wine vinegar just to cover the seeds,
plus a little salt and any flavouring you fancy: honey, crushed green
peppercorns, sesame seeds, ground chillies, tarragon, horseradish. Mix
well, then cover the jar and leave to steep for a week at room temperature.

Drain off the excess liquor, give the mustard a good stir and pack into
cleaned sterilised jars. Seal well and store in a cool place. The mustard will
keep well for 6 months before opening. After that it should be used up
quickly.

Once you have mastered the technique, you can begin to make larger
quantities and give jars to your friends.

HORSERADISH SAUCE

A glance at the label on most bottles of commercial horseradish sauce will reveal a list of ingredients likely to include turnip, colouring, preservatives and emulsifiers. It is usually argued that horseradish sauce will not keep satisfactorily unless it contains these additives. Tuddy Holles has proved that this is nonsense and produces additive-free horseradish sauce as a one-woman cottage industry in Essex. Tuddy's superb horseradish sauce *does* keep, thanks largely to the vinegar.

If you want to make horseradish sauce, the first job is to find the plants. In summer you look for the distinctive shiny green leaves. Tuddy, who learned her craft in childhood, goes out in early spring, marking out the good spots when there's hardly a leaf shoot to be seen. To get the root out of the ground, you need a bit of muscle power. Watching Tuddy work, it's clear a spade is the tool for the job, although a fork is useful for loosening the soil around the roots. Once you have enough root, you will need to wash each piece, peel it, then grate or mince it. The best way is to use an old-fashioned hand-mincer. Horseradish produces tear-inducing vapours, so work in the open air if possible.

The secret of Tuddy's horseradish sauce is not only the freshness of the root, but the 'mayonnaise'. Make the sauce as follows:

Makes about 1½ pints (900 ml)

½ tablespoon (½×15 ml spoon) salt
1 tablespoon (1×15 ml spoon) sugar
½ tablespoon (½×15 ml spoon) dry mustard
1 heaped tablespoon (1×15 ml spoon) cornflour
1 egg, beaten
1 pint (600 ml) milk
10 fl oz (300 ml) malt vinegar

Mix the salt, sugar, mustard and cornflour together in a large, heatproof bowl and blend in the egg. Stir in the milk, then add the vinegar very slowly, stirring constantly. Sit the bowl in a saucepan of water, put on a low heat and cook gently until it thickens, stirring to remove any lumps. Remove from the heat and set aside to cool.

Add some of the 'mayonnaise' to the minced horseradish, until you have a thick flavoursome sauce. Pack into clean, sterilised jars and store in a cool place. Any 'mayonnaise' left over can be kept in the fridge without spoiling.

HORSERADISH VINEGAR

This vinegar needs to be made with freshly grated horseradish root, otherwise the flavour is dull and musty. Find a decent clump and dig up a good root, then wash, peel and either grate it or put it through a mincer (this is a job best done in the open air).

Makes about 1 pint (600 ml)

2 tablespoons (2×15 ml spoons) grated fresh horseradish
1 onion, chopped
1 pint (600 ml) cider vinegar

Pack the grated horseradish and onion into a jar. Heat the vinegar, then pour over. When the jar has cooled, cover and give it a good shake, then let it stand in a warm place for about 6 weeks, shaking it occasionally.

Taste the vinegar after the 6 weeks: if it is sufficiently flavoured, strain it off and re-bottle it; otherwise let it stand for a few weeks more. Store in a cool, dark place when ready for use.

GARLIC VINEGAR

The flavour and intensity of this vinegar is a matter of personal taste, but the quantities listed below suit most palates. A similar vinegar can be made using shallots, using four shallots per 1 pint (600 ml) vinegar.

Makes about 1 pint (600 ml)

6 cloves garlic, sliced
1 pint (600 ml) cider vinegar or white-wine vinegar

Place the garlic in a jar or bottle. Boil the vinegar and pour it hot on to the garlic. When the jar has cooled, cover and give it a good shake, then let it stand for about 1 month in a warm place, shaking it occasionally.

Taste the vinegar after the month: if it is sufficiently flavoured, it can be strained off and re-bottled ready for use. If not, leave it for another couple of weeks, then taste again.

TARRAGON VINEGAR

Herb vinegars are extremely versatile and are definitely worth making if you grow your own herbs. They add a whole new range of flavours to salad dressings, sauces and even pickles. Tarragon vinegar is one of the most successful, but it's worth experimenting with others: choose herbs that have firm stems so they can be put into the jar as decoration. Rosemary, sage, thyme, savory, different types of mint, basil and even lavender are all possibilities. The method is the same in each case—although basil vinegar is likely to be ready within two weeks.

Makes about 1 pint (600 ml)

2 oz (50 g) fresh French tarragon sprigs
1 pint (600 ml) white-wine vinegar

Gather the tarragon just before it blossoms, when the flavour and fragrance are at their peak. Strip off the leaves and pack into a glass jar or bottle. Cover with cold wine vinegar and leave the tarragon to steep for about 1 month. Then strain into a new bottle and add a sprig of fresh tarragon for decoration and extra flavour. Cover and store in a cool, dark place.

BLACKCURRANT VINEGAR

Makes about 2 pints (1.2 litres)

3 lb (1.5 kg) blackcurrants
2 pints (1.2 litres) white-wine vinegar
sugar

Wash the blackcurrants and sort through them, taking out any leaves, stalks and bruised berries. Put into a large bowl and roughly squash the fruit with a wooden spoon. Cover with vinegar and leave for 24–48 hours in a cool place until the vinegar is a good dark colour.

Strain through a jelly bag into a bowl, allowing the juice to drip of its own accord: squeezing the bag will make the vinegar cloudy. Measure the liquid and for each 1 pint (600 ml) add 1 lb (450 g) sugar. Heat gently in a preserving pan for about 10 minutes until the sugar has dissolved. Leave to cool, then bottle, seal and store in a dark place.

RASPBERRY VINEGAR

In the 1920s, raspberry vinegar was a 'refresher', as Lady Jekyll called it, 'suitable for the young after lawn tennis or sports on hot days, but acceptable also to their elders when exhausted by church, depressed by gardening or exasperated by shopping'. More recently it has found its way into the kitchens of chefs dedicated to the new cooking: it now appears as fashionable dressing for salads and in sauces with duck and calves' liver.

Makes about 1 pint (600 ml)

1 lb (450 g) raspberries
1 pint (600 ml) white-wine vinegar
sugar

Sort through the raspberries, throwing out any rotten or blemished fruit. Put into a bowl. Cover with vinegar and leave in a cool larder for 48 hours.

Strain the liquid through a jelly bag into a bowl, allowing the juice to drip of its own accord: squeezing the bag to speed up the process will make the vinegar cloudy. Measure the vinegar and for each 1 pint (600 ml) add 12 oz (350 g) sugar. Place in a preserving pan and boil for 10 minutes until the sugar has dissolved, then set aside to cool. Pour into bottles, seal and store in a dark place. It is ready to use.

NORTH & SOUTH AMERICA

It is said you may still hear the accents of Shakespeare's England in the hills of Virginia, USA. Elsewhere, immigrant Moravians, Italians, Poles, Lutheran Germans, Greeks and Lebanese have created pockets of culture and national tradition in the United States which are often more concentrated and 'authentic' than anything to be found in the mother countries.

Despite its fast-food, high-tech image, America takes its homespun pastimes very seriously indeed. The life-style of *Oklahoma* and *Seven Brides for Seven Brothers*, with its picnics, clam bakes and home-made apple pie is still holding fast in small towns and townships from Maine to Oregon. Even in the cities, where burgers are synonymous with the 'American way', they are often accompanied by traditional tracklements in the shape of dill pickles and mustard relish.

The American Indians were well versed in different ways of preserving their produce—they dried fish and meat, probably did some smoking, and had some other curious tricks as well. The Crees made pemmican by

71

drying thin slices of reindeer or buffalo meat in the sun, then pounding and mixing it with melted fat, which provided nourishment. They picked the fruits growing on their land, such as wild cherries and June berries, and mixed these in to provide extra sweetness. The whole lot was compressed, packed into bags of buffalo hide and kept for five years.

Pickling, as it's known today, began with the arrival of the first English and European settlers, who brought their domestic skills with them. Before long a new tradition had emerged, and all kinds of produce was being salted, brined and pickled in vinegar. Incidentally, the Americans rarely use malt vinegar and consider it something of a luxury. Distilled or cider vinegar are called for in most recipes. The Jewish-American influence is very strong and there are countless recipes for cucumbers, melons, squashes and marrows pickled in various ways. The Americans are also fond of 'freezer' or 'ice box' pickles, which are very mild pickles only intended to keep for a short while with the help of refrigeration.

Pickling in South America and Mexico is rather different. The native Indians had various ingenious ways of preserving food, including a method of drying potatoes in the frost, which seems rather like an ancient precursor of our instant mash! Chilli peppers have been cultivated in parts of South America for 10,000 years and traces of them have been found in ancient burial sites in Ancon and Huaca Pieta in Peru. It's said there are as many varieties of chilli pepper as there are days of the year, so it's not surprising they are extensively pickled and turned into virulent sauces, like their West Indian counterparts. The most popular for pickling are the devilish, tiny green *jalapeño* or *serrano* peppers and the *habanearo* peppers of Brazil and Mexico.

One of the greatest pickles to come out of South America is a style of marinating raw fish in citrus juice, called *ceviche*. The original idea was to find a way of keeping fish in the tropical climate without refrigeration. Also no heat was needed for the preparation or serving: it was cool to make and cool to eat. Traditionally it is made with *corvina* (a member of the Drum family), although cod and haddock are more familiar substitutes in Britain. The fish is steeped in the juice of a special sour orange, although lemon and lime juice are often used instead, and the whole dish is usually spiked up with a couple of hot chillies. In its basic form this is really a peasant fish salad, but the idea has inspired many of today's young chefs. Tim Reeson, of The Crown at Southwold, in Suffolk, has transformed it into a brilliant modern British dish by using turbot, brill and scallops, colouring them with saffron and adding an occasional touch of fresh coriander for effect.

SWEET-AND-SOUR PICKLED MARROW

'What happens when you find that the anaemic little courgette you refrained from picking yesterday has swelled overnight into an enormous *courge* or giant marrow? Of course, you can scoop out the middle and then grate the flesh. Sprinkle it well with salt and leave it to drain in a colander, underneath several weights. Within an hour you will have transformed your swollen monster back into succulent courgettes, which you can mix with beaten eggs and a little flour, for an exotic sort of crêpe. You will also have a large quantity of green juice which can be added to soup stock. You can also use the grated marrow by mixing it with chopped onions and frying it briefly in olive oil or butter.

If you have neglected the garden for a couple of days, only to discover a veritable bounty of marrows, here is a pickle which is a grand accompaniment to cold spreads or curries.'

(*'Cocottes' Norfolk Recipes* by Carla Phillips, The Paper Press, 1982)

This pickle was one of the great 'hits' with everyone involved in the TV series. Like Carla, it is part north Norfolk and part transatlantic. Try it with pâtés and terrines, or you can make a 'good lunch' of it with cottage cheese and bread.

Makes about 2½ lb (1.25 kg)

2½ lb (1.25 kg) marrow
4 onions, sliced
2 green peppers, de-seeded and chopped
2 teaspoons (2×5 ml spoons) salt
10 fl oz (300 ml) cider vinegar
1 lb (450 g) sugar
½ teaspoon (1×2.5 ml spoon) celery seeds
½ teaspoon (1×2.5 ml spoon) white mustard seeds

Split the marrow in half, remove the pulp and pips in the middle and finely slice the flesh. Put into a bowl with the onions and green peppers. Sprinkle with salt and transfer to a large sieve or colander. Press down with a weight and allow to drain for at least 1 hour.

Pour the vinegar into a large pan and add the sugar. Stir well over a low heat until the sugar has dissolved. Add the spices and bring to the boil. Stir in the vegetables, bring to the boil again and cook for about 4 minutes, until the marrow looks translucent. Spoon the pickle into warmed jars or a large plastic container with a lid.

The pickle is ready to eat the next day, but will keep well for up to 3 months.

MELON PICKLE (1)

Davilia David's favourite recipe, gleaned from her favourite recipe book, *The Golden Wattle Cookery Book*. It is Australian, but has echoes of similar pickles made in the USA. Use honeydew or similar varieties of melon.

Makes about 5 lb (2.25 kg)

3 lb (1.5 kg) melon, peeled, de-seeded and diced
1 pint (600 ml) white vinegar
2 lb (1 kg) onions, sliced
1 tablespoon (1×15 ml spoon) salt
8 oz (225 g) white sugar
4 oz (100 g) brown sugar
1½ oz (40 g) fresh root ginger, peeled and finely chopped
1 teaspoon (1×5 ml spoon) ground mixed spice
1 teaspoon (1×5 ml spoon) dill seeds
½ teaspoon (1×2.5 ml spoon) cayenne pepper
2 teaspoons (2×5 ml spoons) turmeric
2 teaspoons (2×5 ml spoons) dry mustard
1 tablespoon (1×15 ml spoon) plain flour

Put the melon in a bowl and cover with vinegar. Leave overnight.

Next day, transfer to a large pan and add the onions, salt, sugars, ginger, mixed spice, dill seeds and cayenne pepper. Boil for about 1 hour until soft. Blend the turmeric and mustard with the flour and mix well with a little water until a smooth paste is formed. Stir into the pickle. Cook slowly, stirring well, until the pickle has thickened and the melon pieces are soft, but still firm. Pack into jars, seal and store for at least 2 months before opening. Age improves it greatly.

MELON PICKLE (2)

This is based on a recipe entitled 'Cantaloupe Pickle', from *The American Heritage Cookbook* (American Heritage, 1964).

Makes about 2½ lb (1.25 kg)

1 large, unripe Cantaloupe melon, peeled, de-seeded and diced
1 pint (600 ml) cider vinegar
1 lb (450 g) dark brown sugar
8 cloves
½ teaspoon (1×2.5 ml spoon) ground cinnamon
½ teaspoon (1×2.5 ml spoon) ground mace

Put the melon into a bowl, cover with the vinegar and leave for 1 hour.

Strain off the vinegar into a saucepan, add the sugar, cloves, cinnamon and mace and bring to the boil. When the sugar has dissolved add the melon and simmer over a low heat for about 15 minutes, or until the pieces are soft and almost transparent.

Lift out the melon pieces with a slotted spoon and pack into warmed jars. Continue to boil the pickling liquid for about another 12 minutes, until it is thick and syrupy. Pour over the melon while hot. Seal and store for 1 week before using. This pickle will keep well for at least 2 months.

SOUR FERMENTED CUCUMBERS

There are countless ways of pickling a small cucumber. Often the recipes are virtually identical, but committed cucumber picklers have a passion about their craft usually reserved for the bedroom rather than the kitchen.

For this American-Jewish pickle you will need cucumbers 4–5 inches (10–12.5 cm) long at most and as firm as sticks of Blackpool rock. They are readily available in the summer and autumn in good greengrocers or markets. In the winter, such cucumbers, imported from the Mediterranean, look bright green and shiny because they have been coated with a fine waxen film. This can make pickling a bit tricky, as the salt will not penetrate. The answer is to grow your own: two grow-bags and a packet of seed, plus patience and green fingers should yield a crop worth pickling.

The ideal receptacle for this pickle is a deep earthenware crock, but a plastic tub will serve just as well.

Makes about 4 pints (2.25 litres)

30 small green cucumbers
brine made of 1 tablespoon (1×15 ml spoon) salt to 1 pint (600 ml) water
1 pint (600 ml) white vinegar
6 tablespoons (6×15 ml spoons) salt
1 teaspoon (1×5 ml spoon) white mustard seeds per jar
5 cloves garlic per jar
1 teaspoon (1×5 ml spoon) dill seeds per jar
2 sprigs fresh dill per jar

Pack the crock or tub two-thirds full with young cucumbers. Cover with a saucer or plate and weight down firmly. Make up enough brine to cover them and pour it in when cold.

Leave for about 1 week in a warm place. As the pickle starts to ferment, a yeasty scum will start to form on the surface. Skim this off regularly. After 2–3 weeks, fermentation should cease and the cucumbers will be ready for pickling. At this stage it is worth sacrificing one cucumber to test if it is sound. Slit it open: the flesh should be firm, but translucent; anything that is sloppy, soggy or slimy should be thrown out. Your nose will also tell you if all is not well.

Decant the fermented cucumbers and pack into cleaned, sterilised jars. Make up a pickle of the vinegar, 3 pints (1.75 litres) water and the salt. Heat in a saucepan until the salt has dissolved, then leave to cool.

Add the mustard seeds, garlic, dill seeds and fresh dill to the jars, then pour on the cooled vinegar, making sure the cucumbers are completely covered. Seal and store in the refrigerator. The cucumbers will keep well for up to 1 month.

SPICED PEACHES

A splendid, fruity pickle that is perfect with ham, salt beef and smoked fish. The recipe works equally well with fresh ripe apricots.

Makes about 2 lb (1 kg)

2 lb (1 kg) small yellow peaches
12 fl oz (350 ml) cider vinegar or white-wine vinegar
1 lb (450 g) sugar
1 tablespoon (1×15 ml spoon) allspice berries

1 tablespoon (1×15 ml spoon) cloves
1 blade mace
1×2 in (5 cm) stick cinnamon

Immerse the fruit in boiling water for 1 minute, then remove and peel. Either leave the peaches whole or split them in half and remove the stones. Put the vinegar into a large pan and add the sugar. Tie the allspice, cloves, mace and cinnamon in a muslin bag and put into the pan along with the fruit. Bring to the boil, then simmer gently for 5 minutes, moving the fruit around carefully with a wooden spoon.

Remove the fruit and pack into warmed jars. Bring the spiced vinegar back to the boil and continue to cook until thick and syrupy. Remove the spice bag and pour carefully over the fruit, making sure they are completely covered. Seal and store for 1 month before opening.

BRANDIED KUMQUATS

This may not sound like a pickle. Instead of brine or vinegar, the fruit is preserved in alcohol. Many kinds of fresh and dried fruit can be used for this recipe, from damsons and peaches to prunes and apricots. It isn't necessary to buy the finest brandy for preserving.

Makes about 1 lb (450 g)

1 lb (450 g) kumquats
8 oz (225 g) sugar
10 fl oz (300 ml) brandy

Sort out the fruit and discard any that are blemished. Put into a pan and just cover with water. Simmer for about 5 minutes, until the kumquats are soft (test by pricking them with a cocktail stick). Remove the fruit from the pan, allow to drain, then pack into warmed jars.

Add the sugar to the juice and boil hard for 5 minutes until it is reduced, then remove from the heat and add the brandy. Allow to cool, then pour over the fruit, making sure all are completely covered. Seal well and store in a dark place. Shake occasionally and keep for at least 1 month before opening.

SWEETCORN RELISH

This classic American relish can be made very simply from packets of frozen corn kernels.

Makes about 1½ lb (750 g)

1 lb (450 g) sweetcorn kernels
1 green pepper, de-seeded and finely diced
1 red pepper, de-seeded and finely diced
4 oz (100 g) celery, thinly sliced
4 oz (100 g) sugar
2 teaspoons (2×5 ml spoons) salt
2 teaspoons (2×5 ml spoons) dry mustard
1 pint (600 ml) cider vinegar

Cook the corn in slightly salted water until tender. Drain and leave to cool. Blanch the peppers and celery in boiling water for 1 minute, then drain. Put all the vegetables into a preserving pan.

Blend the sugar, salt and mustard with a little of the vinegar to form a thin paste. Add this to the vegetables, then pour in the remaining vinegar, bring to the boil and simmer for about 15 minutes, stirring well. Pour the hot relish into warmed jars, seal and store for 2 weeks before using. This relish should be eaten within 1 month.

RED TOMATO RELISH

No burger or barbecued rib would be complete without some spicy tomato relish. Here's a recipe for the real stuff.

Makes about 3 lb (1.5 kg)

2 lb (1 kg) ripe tomatoes
1 onion, finely chopped
4 oz (100 g) celery, finely chopped
4 oz (100 g) green pepper, de-seeded and finely chopped
5 fl oz (150 ml) cider vinegar
2 teaspoons (2×5 ml spoons) white mustard seeds, crushed
1 teaspoon (1×5 ml spoon) cayenne pepper
4 oz (100 g) white sugar

Scald the tomatoes so that the skins will peel off easily. Roughly chop the flesh and drain off as much excess juice as possible. Put into a preserving pan with the onion, celery and green pepper. Cook gently for 5–10 minutes, adding a little vinegar if the mixture starts to dry out. Then add the mustard seeds, cayenne pepper, sugar and remaining vinegar and continue to cook slowly for at least 30 minutes, until the relish is thick and pulpy. Add extra vinegar if the mixture starts to dry out before it is the correct consistency. When ready, pour the relish into warmed jars, seal and store for 2 weeks before eating. It should keep well for 2 months.

CEVICHE (1)

The immense popularity of Mexican food has helped to introduce many people in Britain to ceviche. It's a simple idea and very easy to make at home; it is also very cheap if you use basic firm white fish such as cod or haddock. The recipe is flexible: you can marinate the fish with lemon or lime juice—or a mixture of both; you can spike it with chillies if you like some heat, and you can flavour it with fresh coriander.

Serve the ceviche as a salad, surrounded by colourful vegetables such as sweetcorn, green and red peppers and tomatoes.

Makes about 1 lb (450 g)

1 lb (450 g) white fish fillets, such as cod or haddock, skinned and cut into even-size cubes
1 teaspoon (1×5 ml spoon) salt
1 clove garlic, finely chopped
1 fresh green chilli, de-seeded and finely chopped
juice of 2 lemons or limes
2 teaspoons (2×5 ml spoons) finely chopped fresh coriander

Put the fish into a dish and sprinkle with salt. Mix the garlic and chilli in with the fish, then add the lemon or lime juice and sprinkle with fresh coriander. Cover and leave in the refrigerator for at least 12 hours. The ceviche is then ready to eat and will be good for up to 3 days.

CEVICHE (2)

The idea of ceviche—the marinating of raw fish in citrus juice—has inspired some young British chefs. Tim Reeson, formerly of The Crown, Southwold, Suffolk, makes it regularly and sometimes colours the fish with saffron as an extra touch. The result is dazzling.

It is *essential* that the fish is absolutely fresh. In addition to salmon and turbot, this recipe works well with brill, monkfish, sea bass and even scallops.

Makes about 1¼ lb (500 g)

10 oz (275 g) fresh salmon fillet, skinned
10 oz (275 g) fresh turbot fillet, skinned
1 teaspoon (1×5 ml spoon) salt
½ teaspoon (1×2.5 ml spoon) cumin seeds
½ teaspoon (1×2.5 ml spoon) ground black pepper
3 bay leaves
4 fresh green chillies, de-seeded and finely chopped
handful of chopped fresh coriander
grated rind and juice of 3 limes
grated rind and juice of 2 lemons
virgin olive oil
fresh chives and red pepper strips, to garnish (optional)

Lay the fish side by side in a shallow bowl. Sprinkle with salt. Strew cumin seeds, black pepper, bay leaves, chillies and coriander over the fish. Add the grated rinds and juices of the lemons and limes then dribble a little virgin olive oil over the fish: this helps to keep it moist and prevents the surface from drying out.

Cover and put into the refrigerator to marinate for 6–8 hours, turning the fish every hour. After 8 hours it will be quite strongly flavoured; after that it is likely to become too acidic.

The ceviche should be sliced very thinly like smoked salmon and fanned out prettily on the plate. It can be garnished with chives and very fine strips of red pepper for colour.

THE CARIBBEAN

'The one so like a child's corall, as not to be discerned at the distance of two paces, a crimson and scarlet mixt; the fruit about three inches long and shines more than the best pollisht corall. The other, of the same colour and glistening as much but shaped like a large button of a cloak; both of one and the same quality; both violently strong and growing on a little shrub no bigger than a gooseberry bush.' These words come from Lignon's *History of the Barbadoes*, written between 1647 and 1653. He is talking about chilli peppers—peppers that 'burn the mouth'.

We had first hand experience of the devastating effects of *Capsicum frutescens* when we visited Dounne Moore in her flat in East Ham, London. She imports peppers direct from her native Trinidad and uses them for a unique preparation: Gramma's Pepper Sauce. This highly concentrated condiment, enhanced with a dozen or more herbs, comes in four strengths: mild ('That's hot'), hot ('That's very hot'), extra hot ('That's extremely hot'), and super hot ('That's just unbelievably hot'). The recipe and all the little tricks of the trade were gleaned from Dounne's much-loved grandmother during her Trinidad childhood.

These sauces are used in tiny quantities as condiments on the side of the plate or as flavourings for all kinds of meat, fish and noodle dishes. Impressive claims are also made for their medicinal properties: they are high in vitamins and minerals, they improve the digestion, stimulate the circulation and alleviate rheumatism, chilblains, skin diseases and much more. There is even a West Indian therapeutic pickle called Mandram, consisting of chilli pods mixed with thinly sliced, unpeeled cucumber, shallots, chives or onions, lemon or lime juice and Madeira. It is claimed to work wonders with a weak digestion.

Chilli peppers are also the most common ingredient of more conventional West Indian pickles, along with sweet peppers, carrots and cho-cho—a curious vegetable that looks like a cross between a pear and a gourd. To say these pickles are very hot is an understatement. The look of sheer ecstatic agony on Davilia's face as she braved her first tiny mouthful of Mayblin Hamilton's pickled peppers said it all!

PICKLED HOT PEPPERS

Make no mistake: this pickle is one of the hottest and most powerful you are ever likely to taste. The devastating heat comes from special West Indian peppers that look a bit like wrinkled snooker balls; look for them at Indian and Caribbean shops and markets. Mayblin Hamilton, of the Plantation Inn, Leytonstone, London, who devised this recipe, makes it look pretty by carving some of the pieces of vegetables into sunny smiling faces with big grins. Cho-cho is a pale green, pear-shaped vegetable related to the marrow. It is also known as chow-chow, chayote and christophene, and is available from Caribbean markets and shops, fresh and in tins.

Makes about 2 lb (1 kg)

12 hot red peppers, red and yellow
2 onions, thinly sliced
3×2 inch (5 cm) strips carrot, peeled
1×2 inch (5 cm) strip cho-cho, peeled
1 tablespoon (1×15 ml spoon) allspice berries
1 teaspoon (1×5 ml spoon) salt
1 pt (600 ml) white vinegar

Wash the peppers, remove the stems and cut the flesh of each into 4 strips lengthwise. Pack the strips into a large sterilised jar. Add the onions to the jar. Arrange the carrot and cho-cho strips around the outside of the jar so they look attractive. Add the allspice and salt, then cover with vinegar, filling the jar to the top. Seal and leave for 24 hours before using.

A word of warning: handle the peppers with great care, and wash your hands thoroughly as soon as you have finished slicing and packing. Don't touch your face and eyes until you have done so.

PICKLISES

The information for this Haitian recipe comes from *Caribbean Cookery* by Elisabeth Lambert Ortiz (André Deutsch, 1975). It is one of those good working pickle recipes without precise ingredients. You start with any vegetables that are to hand: equal quantities of, say, chopped French beans, finely shredded cabbage, cauliflower florets, carrots cut into thin slices, onions, green peas, sliced radishes, celery, plus the obligatory hot red peppers pricked with a fork. Pack everything into a large crock or jar. Cover with white vinegar and leave to stand in a cool place at least 1 week. The pickle is served with steak or roast meat, or with biscuits, cheese and drinks. It will keep in the refrigerator for about 1 week.

HOT-PEPPER SAUCE (1)

Every family in every town in the Caribbean seems to have its own recipe for hot-pepper sauce. Here is an all-purpose version that will blister the taste-buds, spike up soups and stews and clear the brain after a heavy night's drinking.

Makes about 6 fl oz (175 ml)

3 fresh hot red peppers, de-seeded and finely chopped
1 onion, finely chopped
2 cloves garlic, finely chopped
4 fl oz (120 ml) white-wine vinegar
1 teaspoon (1×5 ml spoon) salt
1 tablespoon (1×15 ml spoon) vegetable oil

Put the peppers into a bowl with the onion and garlic. Put the vinegar, salt and 4 fl oz (120 ml) water in a saucepan, bring to the boil and pour hot over the pepper mixture. Stir well.

Leave until cold, then purée in a blender or food processor and pack into a cleaned, sterilised bottle. Finally add the oil, drop by drop, so it forms a sealing layer on top of the sauce.

The sauce will keep well for at least 1 month, particularly if stored in the refrigerator.

HOT-PEPPER SAUCE (2)

This recipe is bulked out with cho-cho (see p. 153).

Makes about 12 fl oz (350 ml)

1 cho-cho
2 tablespoons (2×15 ml spoons) vegetable oil
1 onion, finely chopped
3 cloves garlic, finely chopped
2 spring onions, finely chopped
6 fresh hot red peppers, de-seeded and finely chopped
10 fl oz (300 ml) white-wine vinegar
1 teaspoon (1×5 ml spoon) salt

Put the cho-cho in a saucepan of water and simmer for about 20 minutes until soft. Drain, peel and roughly chop the flesh. Meanwhile, heat the oil in a pan. Add the onions, garlic and spring onions and fry until the onions become yellow and translucent.

Purée the onion mixture, cho-cho and peppers in a blender, adding the vinegar gradually until you have a smooth sauce. Season with salt. Pack into warm, sterilised bottles or jars and store in the refrigerator. The sauce keeps well for up to 1 month.

PUMPKIN CHUTNEY

A simple, spicy chutney devised by Mayblin Hamilton of the Plantation Inn, Leytonstone, London. The ginger and hot red peppers give it a typically Caribbean punch.

Makes about 2½ lb (1.25 kg)

1 lb (450 g) pumpkin, peeled, trimmed and diced
10 fl oz (300 ml) malt vinegar
1 lb (450 g) light or dark brown sugar
3 hot red peppers, de-seeded and finely chopped
1 oz (25 g) fresh root ginger, peeled and finely chopped
1 oz (25 g) garlic, finely chopped
4 oz (100 g) onions, finely chopped
4 oz (100 g) raisins, finely chopped
1 tablespoon (1×15 ml spoon) salt

Put the pumpkin into a pan with 1 pint (600 ml) water, bring to the boil, then cook for about 15 minutes until tender.

Add the vinegar and sugar to the pumpkin, stir well and bring to the boil. When the sugar has dissolved, add the peppers, ginger, garlic, onions, raisins and salt and cook rapidly for 35–45 minutes, stirring well. Leave to cool, then pack into warm jars, and store in a cool place for a couple of months before opening.

GREEN PAW-PAW CHUTNEY

Paw-paw, or papaya, is a tropical fruit not unlike mango: it is green when unripe, yellow when ripe. This recipe can be used for green mangoes too.

Makes about 2 lb (1 kg)

2 lb (1 kg) green, unripe paw-paw, peeled and cut into 1 inch (2.5 cm) cubes
8 oz (225 g) sultanas, rinsed and coarsely chopped
2 oz (50 g) fresh root ginger, peeled and chopped
2 cloves garlic, chopped
2 fresh hot red peppers, de-seeded and finely chopped
1 pint (600 ml) malt vinegar
1 lb (450 g) light brown sugar
pinch of salt

Put the paw-paw, sultanas, ginger, garlic and peppers into a large pan with the vinegar. Stir well together and simmer for about 15 minutes. Warm the sugar, then add it to the mixture and simmer for a further 15 minutes or until the chutney has thickened. Add salt to taste.

Pack the hot chutney into warm sterilised jars, seal and store at least 2 months before using.

ESCOVITCH FISH

This is the pure West Indian version of Escabeche (see p. 115), given to us by Mayblin Hamilton of the Plantation Inn, Leytonstone, London. It is often eaten for Sunday breakfast, with 'bammies' (round white bread made with cassava flour), hard dough bread, Johnny cakes (deep-fried dumplings) and fresh lemonade.

4×8 oz (225 g) fish (snapper and red mullet are best)
juice of 2 limes
salt and freshly ground black pepper
vegetable oil
1–2 cho-chos, peeled and cut in 2 inch (5 cm) strips
1–2 carrots, peeled and cut in 2 inch (5 cm) strips
2 onions, sliced
2 green peppers, de-seeded and cut in 2 inch (5 cm) strips
2 hot red peppers, de-seeded and sliced
2 bay leaves
2 tablespoons (2×15 ml spoons) allspice berries
10 fl oz (300 ml) white-wine vinegar

Clean and gut the fish, keeping them whole. Rub with lime juice, then pat dry with a cloth. Sprinkle them, inside and out, with salt and pepper. Heat plenty of oil in a pan (it should be at least 1 inch (2.5 cm) deep) until it begins to smoke. Place the fish in the hot oil, one at a time, taking care that they do not overlap. Reduce the heat and fry for a few minutes on each side. When the fish are cooked, lift them out, drain well and arrange on a large platter.

Put the cho-chos, carrots, onions, peppers, bay leaves and allspice in a saucepan with the vinegar. Bring to the boil, then simmer for 2 minutes. Remove from the heat and pour the hot pickle over the fish. The mixture should be left to marinate for 24 hours, and will keep up to 3 days in the fridge. It can be served hot or cold.

HOT-PEPPER VINEGAR

Here's an extremely powerful condiment that can be used, drop by drop, in soups and sauces. It is best put into a bottle with a dropper at the top—an empty Angostura bitters bottle is perfect. Replace the vinegar with dry sherry or light rum and you have a very different, alcoholic condiment that can be used in the same way.

Makes about 1 pint (600 ml)

6 whole fresh hot red peppers, or 2 oz (50 g) dried red peppers
1 pint (600 ml) white-wine vinegar

Put the fresh or dried peppers whole into a bottle or jar. Pour in the white-wine vinegar, shake well, cork and leave for at least 4 weeks. The vinegar will continue to mature for at least 6 months—in fact there are stories of legendary bottles matured for 25 years.

SCANDINAVIA & NORTHERN EUROPE

The earliest methods of preserving meat and fish—and to a certain extent fruit and vegetables—relied on the seasons, the elements and natural resources. In Southern Europe, this meant salt, sun and oil. In the North, a good steady north-easterly blow might do the trick, plus some salty spray and wood smoke. In Iceland and many other parts of Scandinavia, the wind-drying of cod and haddock, split open and laid on racks or 'stocks', still produces supplies of 'stockfish', a food with the consistency of chipboard and the aroma of a teenage boy's socks. The secret is lots of butter and strong jaws—then it's delicious. When the weather becomes too warm, the curers move over to 'klipfish', cod that is first salted, then dried on the rocks or 'klippe'.

The Scandinavians have also refined ways of curing fish, particularly herring and salmon, which set the pickling standard for the rest of the world. From the Middle Ages onwards, the herring industry was quite literally the backbone of the economy of half a dozen North European countries—Holland, Germany and the Scandinavian countries, not to mention parts of England and Scotland. Before ice, refrigeration and fast transport, virtually all the catch had to be preserved by pickling or smoking. Barrels of pickled 'white' herring and smoked 'reds' were shipped by the boatload from one European port to another. But the pickling of herring wasn't simply a commercial trade: it was an essential domestic craft as well.

Away from her native Sweden, the uncrowned queen of the pickled herring is Anna Hegarty, who owns Anna's Place in Stoke Newington, North London, and puts on her special show for delighted customers night after night. She showed us the making of the classic pickled herring, and also the famous 'Three Kinds of Herring'—a dish that struck a chord in our memories of Reykjavik and Oslo. In this speciality, the salt-cured fish is prepared with sugar and wine, with mustard and dill, and with mild curried mayonnaise, then eaten with dark rye bread and unsalted butter.

Anna's greatest triumph, though, is *gravadlax* (*gravlax* in Danish). We think her version of this method of salting and marinating salmon is unequalled in England. Fifteen years ago you would be hard pressed to find it anywhere in Britain; these days it is elbowing its close cousin, smoked salmon, from restaurant menus across the land. The word *gravadlax* means literally 'buried salmon', and refers to the ancient practice of preserving fish in pits. When fishermen were far from home, they would pack sides of salmon between layers of birch bark and fir branches, weight them down with stones and bury them in a pit on the shore or in the cold Scandinavian earth. Later the fish were salted first, then stored in a kind of underground larder reinforced with rocks or a heavy wooden door.

Salmon *is* a luxury, but there are other, cheaper fish that will do the trick. Bernard Phillips of the Moorings Restaurant at Wells-next-the-Sea on the Norfolk coast showed us it is possible to make an imitation—a 'poor man's *gravlax*'—with grey mullet, sea bass or even trout. The setting for this may be English, but the style and inspiration are from Scandinavia.

But there's more to pickling in Scandinavia and Northern Europe than fish. The Germans have *sauerkraut*, a classic speciality of salted and fermented cabbage, which is virtually their national dish. Elsewhere, there are dill-pickled cucumbers, baby beetroots lightly pickled and garnished with caraway seeds, mushrooms and tomatoes. We have even sampled a kind of sweet pickled broccoli as part of a Danish breakfast.

There's no better description of pickles and preserves on the Swedish table than this litany of good things, described by the French traveller

Paul du Chaillu in 1871. He was in Gotenburg:

'I was led to a little table, called smorgasbord, around which we all clus-
tered and upon which I saw a display of smoked reindeer meat, cut into
small thin slices; smoked salmon with poached eggs; fresh raw sliced
salmon, called graflax, upon which salt had been put about an hour
before; hard-boiled eggs; caviare; fried sausage; a sort of anchovy, caught
on the western coast; raw, salted Norwegian herring, exceedingly fat, cut
into small pieces; sillsalat, made of pickled herring; small pieces of boiled
meat, potato etc. with olive oil, and vinegar; smoked goose-breast;
cucumbers, soft brown and white bread, cut into small slices; knackebrod,
a sort of flat, hard bread made of coarse rye flour and flavoured with ani-
seed; siktadt bread, very thin, and made of the finest bolted flour; butter;
gammal ost, the strongest old cheese one can taste, and kummin ost, a
cheese seasoned with caraway; three crystal decanters, containing different kinds of branvin [spirits]; renadt, made from rye or potatoes;
pomerans, made from renadt, with the addition of oil or bitter orange and
somewhat sweet, and finkelbranvin, or unpurified spirit.'

(Quoted in *European Peasant Cookery* by Elisabeth Luard, Bantam
Press, 1986, Corgi, 1988)

PICKLED HERRING (1)

The Scandinavians still have a great fondness for pickled herring, and
each family seems to have its own special recipe. These days the starting
point is usually salted and skinned herring fillets, which can be bought in
cans or tubs from specialist delicatessens and Scandinavian food stores
(see Appendix).

Once pickled, the herring can be used in countless ways. A glance
through any Scandinavian recipe book will provide you with scores of
ideas for salads, garnishes and dressings.

Makes about 2 lb (1 kg)

2 lb (1 kg) salt herring fillets
3 red onions, sliced
10 fl oz (300 ml) white vinegar
2 tablespoons (2×15 ml spoons) sugar
2 bay leaves
2 teaspoons (2×5 ml spoons) juniper berries

2 teaspoons (2×5 ml spoons) allspice berries
1 teaspoon (1×5 ml spoon) black peppercorns

Remove the fillets from their liquor, then soak overnight in a bowl of cold water.

Next day, drain the fillets and pat dry. Arrange in a dish and cover with red onions, which add colour as well as flavour.

Heat the vinegar with 10 fl oz (300 ml) water in a saucepan and add the sugar and bay leaves, juniper berries, allspice berries and peppercorns. Bring to the boil and cook for 10 minutes. Leave to cool, then pour the spiced vinegar over the fish and onions, making sure they are completely covered. Leave in a cool place for at least 48 hours before serving. These herring will keep for up to a month in the fridge, provided they are always covered with vinegar.

PICKLED HERRING (2)

This recipe is for pickling small fresh herring. They are not salted before pickling, so the dish is only intended to keep for about 3 days.

Makes about 2 lb (1 kg)

2 lb (1 kg) fresh herring
2 teaspoons (2×5 ml spoons) salt
1 tablespoon (1×15 ml spoon) sugar
1 teaspoon (1×5 ml spoon) white mustard seeds
1 teaspoon (1×5 ml spoon) black peppercorns
1 pint (600 ml) white vinegar
4 tablespoons (4×15 ml spoons) chopped fresh dill

It is worth knowing how to prepare and fillet a whole herring: scrape off any loose scales, then cut off the head and tail, split open the belly and remove the guts. Next, take out the backbone. Put the fish belly-side down on a board and press along the whole length of the back with your thumb, then turn the fish over and ease the backbone away from the flesh with a knife; most of the smaller bones will come away as well. Rinse the fish and drain well on a cloth.

Put the salt, sugar, mustard seeds, peppercorns and vinegar in a pan, bring to the boil and simmer for 10 minutes, then set aside to cool.

Line the bottom of a deep dish with a layer of dill, then arrange some fish on top, fleshy sides down. Sprinkle more dill on top and add another layer of fish, finishing with a layer of dill. Pour over the cold spiced vinegar, making sure the fish are completely covered. Stand the dish in a cool place for at least 24 hours and up to 48 hours, depending on how strong a pickle you like. The herrings are then ready for eating.

PICKLED HERRING (3)

Another Scandinavian variation on the theme: this time the starting point is cooked herring. It is a good way of preserving any leftovers from a fresh herring feast.

Makes about 2 lb (1 kg)

2 onions, sliced
2 lb (1 kg) whole herring, cooked
2 tablespoons (2×15 ml spoons) sugar
2 bay leaves
2 teaspoons (2×5 ml spoons) allspice berries
1 pint (600 ml) white vinegar
sprigs of fresh dill or fennel

Arrange the onions on the bottom of a large shallow dish and put the herring carefully on top, preferably in a single layer.

Put the sugar, bay leaves and allspice in a pan with the vinegar, bring to the boil and simmer for 10 minutes, then set aside to cool. Pour the cold pickle over the fish, making sure they are completely covered. Leave for 24 hours before using. Scatter sprigs of fresh dill or fennel over the dish just before serving. This pickle should be consumed within 3 days.

SCANDINAVIAN SPICED HERRINGS

Gaffelbitar, or herring tit-bits, are bite-sized morsels of salted and spiced fish. They are one of Scandinavia's favourite foods and have something of a following in Britain and the USA as well. They have only been produced in their present form since 1906, when a man named Alfred Bovik had the notion of packing herring in barrels on board ship with a special mixture of salt, sugar and spices. He provided the captains of the boats fishing off Iceland with bags of his mixture and instructions as to how it should be used. Then he waited. The result was a prototype of *gaffelbitar*.

This method of curing produces a transformation: the fish looks more like an obscure sort of raw ham, the flesh is soft, pink and succulent, and the aroma is curiously exquisite. In practice *gaffelbitar* can only be produced successfully on a large scale, some of the original recipes calling for Spanish hops and sandalwood, and the process is still very time consuming. It is possible, however, to make a very passable imitation at home using the following recipe. It is worth trying, because there are so many ways of serving the fish: they are perfect with crisp radishes and rye bread; they can be used to top all kinds of open sandwiches; they go well with pickled dill cucumbers; and can be made into salads with apples, potatoes, onions and any kind of creamy dressing.

12 fresh herring fillets
10 fl oz (300 ml) white vinegar
4 oz (100 g) sugar
2 oz (50 g) sea salt
2 teaspoons (2×5 ml spoons) allspice berries
2 teaspoons (2×5 ml spoons) black peppercorns
1 onion, sliced
2 tablespoons (2×15 ml spoons) chopped fresh dill

Clean the herring fillets and leave them to dry on a cloth. Mix 2 pints (1.2 litres) water and the vinegar together and soak the herring for a couple of hours. Meanwhile, crush the sugar, salt, allspice and peppercorns roughly using a pestle and mortar.

Rinse the herring and drain them well, rub them all over with the salt and spice mixture. Sprinkle the bottom of a deep dish or crock with some of the salt mixture, then pack in some herring—skin side upwards— onion slices and dill in layers, sprinkling more of the salt between the layers. Finish with a layer of onion and a final sprinkling of salt.

Cover the dish and stand it in a cool place for at least 24 hours and up to 48 hours depending on how strong a pickle you like. The fish are then ready for use. If stored in the fridge, they will remain good for about 5 days.

ROLLMOP HERRING

Rollmops are famous throughout Scandinavia and Germany. They are also well known in Britain, although most commercial versions sold in pubs and delicatessens are an acidic travesty of the real thing. At its best, a rollmop is one of the finest kinds of pickled herring; it needs only some potatoes and a green salad as accompaniments.

6 herring
2 oz (50 g) salt
2 bay leaves
1 teaspoon (1×5 ml spoon) cloves
1 teaspoon (1×5 ml spoon) white mustard seeds
1 teaspoon (1×5 ml spoon) black peppercorns
1 pint (600 ml) white vinegar or cider vinegar
1 onion, thinly sliced
2 pickled dill cucumbers, thinly sliced

Scale the herrings, cut off their heads and tails and gut them thoroughly. Wash well, then remove the backbone (see p. 91), but leave them as double fillets. Make up a brine with the salt and 1 pint (600 ml) water and let the fish soak for about 3 hours.

Make up the pickle by boiling the bay leaves, cloves, mustard seeds and peppercorns in the vinegar for 10 minutes, then set aside to cool.

Remove the fish from the brine and dry well. Roll each fillet around a slice of onion and a slice of pickled cucumber and secure with a toothpick. Pack the rollmops into a straight-sided jar or dish and cover with the cold spiced vinegar, including the bay leaves and spices. Cover and leave in a cool place for 3– 4 days before serving. They will keep well for up to 2 months in the fridge, provided the fish is always covered with vinegar.

BISMARCK HERRING

These were once known as 'saure lappen' or 'sour lobes', because they were made from double fillets of herring opened out like a book. Nowadays they are normally made from single fillets which can be bought from most fishmongers. The simplest way to serve these German-style pickled herrings is to put them in a dish with a little red pepper and onion from the pickle, pour sour cream over them and eat them with potato salad.

6 herring (or 12 herring fillets)
2 oz (50 g) salt
1 teaspoon (1×5 ml spoon) black peppercorns
1 teaspoon (1×5 ml spoon) mustard seeds
2 dried red chillies
1 pint (600 ml) distilled white vinegar
1 onion, sliced
1 red pepper, de-seeded and cut into strips

Get the fishmonger to fillet the fish for you, or follow the method given on p. 91. Mix the salt with 1 pint (600 ml) water, add the herring and set aside to soak for 2–3 hours. Put the peppercorns, mustard seeds and chillies in a pan with the vinegar, bring to the boil and simmer for 10 minutes, then set aside to cool.

Drain the herring and leave on tea-towels to drain. Lay them in a large shallow dish, cover with slices of onion and strips of red pepper, then pour the cold pickle over them. Leave in a cool place for at least 3 days before using. They will keep well in the fridge for up to 2 weeks.

GRAVLAX (1)

This classic method of marinating salmon has been perfected throughout Scandinavia and recipes vary a great deal. Restaurateurs such as Anna Hegarty cure whole fish split into sides, but it is possible to make a perfectly good version using a middle cut or a cheaper tail-end piece.

Clean, scale and bone the salmon, or get the fishmonger to do it for you. Divide into two fillets.

For each 1 lb (450 g) of prepared fish, use the following:
2 tablespoons (2×15 ml spoons) sea salt
1 tablespoon (1×15 ml spoon) sugar
1 tablespoon (1×15 ml spoon) crushed black peppercorns
freshly chopped dill

Lay 1 fillet of fish, skin side downwards, in a shallow stainless steel or glass dish. Grind together the salt, sugar and peppercorns and sprinkle evenly over the fleshy side. Then put on a generous amount of chopped fresh dill. Lay the other fillet on top, skin side upwards.

The fish then needs to be covered with a large plate or wooden board and weighted down. Put in the refrigerator for at least 24 hours or up to 48 hours if the salmon weighs more than 3 lb (1.5 kg): the fish should be turned every 12 hours.

Although the fish is ready to eat after the marinating is complete, it will keep well in the refrigerator for up to 1 week.

To serve, scrape off the salt and spices, and slice the fish thinly like smoked salmon. Alternatively, cut the flesh straight downwards towards the skin in thick chunks. Classically gravlax is eaten with rye bread, potato salad and dill mustard sauce.

GRAVLAX (2)

More economical, but equally interesting versions of gravlax can be made with many different kinds of fish. Bernard Phillips of the Moorings Restaurant, Wells-next-the-Sea, Norfolk, showed us his way with grey mullet and suggested other fish such as sea bass and trout.

The basic idea is the same, but he has a few variations, including skinning the fish and wrapping the fillets in cling film while they are marinating. He also adds brandy to the salt and sugar mixture.

Clean and prepare the fish as above, but also remove the skin.

For each 1 lb (450 g) prepared fish use the following:
2 tablespoons (2×15 ml spoons) sea salt
1 tablespoon (1×15 ml spoon) sugar
freshly chopped dill
1 tablespoon (1×15 ml spoon) brandy

Mix the salt, sugar and dill in a bowl and add enough brandy to form a thick paste. Blend well.

Line a shallow tray or bowl with cling film. Spread some of the salt mixture on it and lay 1 fillet, skinned side down, in the centre. Spread the fish liberally with more of the mixture, then place the second fillet on top, skinned side upwards. Cover with the rest of the mixture. Wrap up the fillets with cling film. Put a plate or weighted board on top and leave in a cool place for at least 24 hours. The fish is best served with a dill mustard sauce, and will keep for up to 1 week in the fridge.

SAUERKRAUT

Fermented, or 'barrel cabbage', is one of the classic Middle European peasant specialities. It is an ancient, seasonal method of preserving aimed at providing supplies of cabbage through the winter and into the spring, when the first green leaves of fresh cabbage re-appear. Sauerkraut is normally made in bulk—50 cabbages at a time, shredded and packed in wooden barrels, and checked every week through the winter to ensure that the stuff isn't spoiling.

This is a scaled down version, for those who are interested and want something special to go with roast pork, sausages or rye bread and sour cream.

Use firm heads of autumn cabbages such as Dutch white, Savoy or drumhead.

Makes about 1½ lb (1.5 kg)

2 lb (1 kg) cabbage
1 oz (25 g) salt
a few caraway seeds

Choose a firm cabbage, wash and remove the outer leaves and stalk. Line a thoroughly cleaned and sterilised jar or earthenware crock with a few leaves. Shred the rest of the cabbage very finely and mix well with the salt and caraway seeds. Pack into the container, pressing the cabbage down hard. Put a few whole leaves on top, then cover. It is essential that the cover rests directly on the cabbage and is weighted down to exclude the air.

Leave the container at room temperature for about 1 week. During this time a brine will form and cover the cabbage. If necessary, top up with more brine: 1 oz (25 g) salt to 2 pints (1.2 litres) water. Soon the cabbage will start to ferment and a foam will start to appear on top. Skim this off periodically. After 2–3 weeks, fermentation should stop and the cabbage will be ready to eat. It should be rinsed and drained well to get rid of excess salt before serving.

PICKLED GREEN TOMATOES

Too many pickle recipes read – and taste – as though they are the last desperate solution to the problem of gluts. Green tomatoes are the classic example. This German recipe calls for green tomatoes 'small enough to eat whole', which means growing them deliberately and picking the clusters of small fruit while they are still green, firm and fresh. One of the best varieties to grow is the cherry tomato called Gardener's Delight. This has the great advantage that the skins of the fruit are unlikely to split.

This is an extraordinary pickle. Once you have tasted it you will never again forget that the tomato really is a fruit. It goes well with cheese, even better with pâtés and terrines.

Makes about 5 lb (2.2 kg)

5 lb (2.25 kg) green tomatoes, 1 inch (2.5 cm) diameter maximum, stems removed
2 pints (1.2 litres) malt vinegar
6 cloves
1×1 inch (2.5 cm) cinnamon stick
½ small nutmeg (or 2 blades mace)
pinch salt
1 lb (450 g) sugar
1 pint (600 ml) white-wine vinegar

Place the tomatoes in a large pan with the malt vinegar. Stir very gently and bring to the boil, then strain immediately. (The malt vinegar can be thrown away or saved for making chutney.) Tip the tomatoes very carefully into a bowl, taking care not to split the skins.

Boil the cloves, cinnamon, nutmeg or mace, salt and sugar with the wine vinegar in a separate pan, then pour hot over the tomatoes. Cover and leave for 24 hours.

Strain off the liquid, boil up again, but this time leave to cool before pouring over the tomatoes. Leave for a further 24 hours.

On the third day, heat the tomatoes and the liquid together, but do not boil. Lift out the tomatoes with a slotted spoon and pack them carefully into warmed jars. Throw out any that have accidentally split their skins because they will ruin the effect of the pickle.

Reduce the liquid until it turns slightly syrupy, then strain off the spices and pour the cooling pickle over the tomatoes, making sure they are completely covered. Cover and store for 3 months before opening.

PICKLED BABY BEETROOT

The Scandinavians are very fond of pickled beetroot: it is a regular feature on the cold table, it is used as a relish for meats, and the pickling liquor is sometimes added to dishes of pickled herrings to give colour and sweetness. This recipe is best made with whole baby beetroots, the size of golf balls. Unlike the English version, this pickle is very light and can be served and eaten the day after it has been made; it isn't intended for long keeping.

10 baby beetroots
5 fl oz (150 ml) cider vinegar
2 oz (50 g) sugar
1 teaspoon (1×5 ml spoon) salt
2 teaspoons (2×5 ml spoons) caraway seeds

Wash the beets well and cook them for 5–10 minutes until just tender, then peel and set aside to cool. Boil the vinegar with 5 fl oz (150 ml) water and the sugar and salt in a pan for 5 minutes, then remove from the heat and set aside to cool.

Pack the beets into a deep bowl or jar and cover with the cold vinegar. Sprinkle with caraway seeds and store in a cool place for a day before using.

SCANDINAVIAN DILL CUCUMBERS

This is Scandinavia's favourite pickled vegetable. It can be made with whole baby cucumbers, 3–4 inches (7.5–10 cm) long, or with thin slices from larger specimens. It makes a perfect summer salad and a fine accompaniment to pickled herring (see p. 90) and other delights on the smorgasbord. This recipe is for sliced cucumbers.

Makes about 8 oz (225 g)

2 cucumbers
2 teaspoons (2×5 ml spoons) salt
2 teaspoons (2×5 ml spoons) sugar
5 fl oz (150 ml) cider vinegar
2 teaspoons (2×5 ml spoons) chopped fresh dill

Wash the cucumbers well to remove any waxy coating which prevents the salt penetrating, then dry well. Cut into thin slices and put into a deep bowl with the salt. Cover with a plate and something heavy, leave in a cool place for 2 hours, then drain well and press out any excess juice.

Dissolve the sugar in the vinegar and pour over the sliced cucumbers. Sprinkle with dill and put into the refrigerator to chill. The pickle is ready to eat the same day, and will keep well for 2–3 days.

PICKLED COCKTAIL OR PEARL ONIONS

There is apparently an old German proverb that says 'sour makes cheerful'. No doubt this reflects a love of sweet-and-sour pickles! The Germans distinguish between *silberzwiebeln* (cocktail onions), which are about hazelnut size, and even smaller pearl onions. Both are pickled in similar fashion.

As an alternative, try using fresh baby sweetcorn instead of onions. These are available in most supermarkets and good greengrocers. Leave them whole, blanch them and follow the recipe given below.

Makes about 1 lb (450 g)

1 lb (450 g) cocktail or pearl onions
10 fl oz (300 ml) white-wine vinegar
2 oz (50 g) sugar
1 teaspoon (1×5 ml spoon) white mustard seeds
1 oz (25 g) fresh root ginger, peeled and thinly sliced

Peel or rub the skins off the onions and plunge into boiling water for about 10 seconds to blanch them. Drain and leave to cool.

Heat the vinegar in a saucepan with the sugar, mustard seeds and ginger and boil for 10 minutes, then remove from the heat and allow to cool.

Pack the onions in cleaned sterilised jars and pour over the vinegar with the spices. Cover and store in a cool place for 1 week before opening. The onions will last well for up to 1 month.

EASTERN EUROPE

The little Jewish gentleman's eyes sparkled as he recounted his mother's recipe for pickled cucumbers. Now he lives alone, but he still makes them the old way for his grandchildren from a recipe that probably had its origins in Poland or the vast open spaces of the Ukraine. It may have been refined by an aunt in Tel Aviv or a second cousin in North London, but here it was in London's Berwick Street market, in the heart of West End, still alive and kicking.

Away from the cosmopolitan garishness of Soho, in Whitechapel is Barry Rogg's Kosher delicatessen—one of the last survivors of a tradition going back generations. Barry's grandfather started the business and Barry has been entrenched in the trade for more than forty years. Here, the pickled cucumber reigns supreme. Every inch of shelf space seems to be taken up with cans and jars of all shapes and sizes; they are stacked high against the walls, arrayed in the windows. Of course, Barry pickles his own, and these are clearly the best-sellers. He does two versions: one a conventional sweet-and-sour pickle using small, knobbly whole gherkins; the other in a very dilute vinegar which produces a mild, almost fermented pickle, with half cucumbers swimming in their liquor.

Until recently, Barry did his pickling in wooden barrels, but now he has switched over to pedal bins and plastic dustbins. When we visited him, he showed us the very last wooden barrel lurking by the shop doorway. In the pickle we could see cucumbers, with bay leaves, red chillies and garlic halves. Barry does a roaring trade: because fewer people are making their own, he sells more of his home-made delicacies than ever before. Not only cucumbers, but pickled green tomatoes and herrings and cured salmon.

Right across Eastern Europe and into Russia, pickling is second nature: 'We pickle because we have to.' The Bulgarians have a great reputation as gardeners and many consider their *torshi*, or pickled vegetables, the finest in the region.

It is a different story in Poland, however, where food shortages are a way of life. Fresh foods—beetroots, tomatoes, cucumbers, pears, mushrooms—are bought in bulk when they are available and pickled so they last. Once the items have been pickled in the normal way, they are sealed using a special steam method which involves putting the jars in a big pan of boiling water until a vacuum is created and the lids are tight. This is pickling out of necessity, not simply for pleasure, although Polish pickles are famous for their particular blend of sweetness and sourness.

In Hungary, the quality of canned and bottled produce is very high, yet there is still some home-pickling and preserving: cucumbers in vinegar, plums in vinegar with cinnamon, and preserved *lecso*—peppers and tomatoes—are still common. Hungarians have a curious variation on the Polish method of steam-sealing: the hot preserves are put into hot jars and kept continuously at 60–70°F (15–19°C) so they cool very slowly. This is done by surrounding the hot jars with blankets, newspapers and cushions and wrapping them up so no cool air can get to them. After a day and a night they are fully preserved.

The Russians use their pickles as *zakuski*, or hors d'oeuvres. There are pickled grapes and mushrooms, salted cucumbers, tomatoes (both green and red) and cabbage fermented rather like *sauerkraut*. All that is needed as the final touch is a glass of vodka!

POLISH PICKLED CUCUMBERS

This version of dill cucumbers is done in a very mild pickle and needs a special 'steam-sealing' technique to help with preservation. After this, the jars can be stored for months without deteriorating, but should be used up quickly once opened. Steam-sealing isn't essential if you intend to consume the cucumbers within 4 weeks. Eat with salt beef, fried fish or Polish dumplings.

Makes about 4½ lb (2 kg)

4½ lb (2 kg) small cucumbers, 4–6 inches (10–15 cm) long
1 clove garlic per jar
1 teaspoon (1×5 ml spoon) black peppercorns per jar
2 bay leaves per jar
1½ teaspoons (3×2.5 ml spoons) dill seeds per jar
10 fl oz (300 ml) white vinegar
2 tablespoons (2×15 ml spoons) sugar
1 tablespoon (1×15 ml spoon) salt

Wash the cucumbers well, dry them and pack vertically into cleaned, sterilised jars. To each jar add a cut clove of garlic, peppercorns, bay leaves and dill seeds.

Heat the vinegar and 2½ pints (1.5 litres) water in a saucepan, add the sugar and salt and boil until dissolved. Leave to cool, then pour over the cucumbers, making sure they are completely covered. Seal.

To steam the jars, get a large pan and line it with a towel (this prevents the jars coming into direct contact with the pan itself). Add plenty of water and bring to the boil. Place the jars in the pan, making sure that the water level is two-thirds of the way up. Allow to boil for 45 minutes. Then check the seal: if it is tight, the jars are ready; if not, repeat the sealing treatment.

CUCUMBERS PICKLED IN BRINE

There are many versions of this pickle throughout Eastern Europe. In Hungary the cucumbers are often flavoured with horseradish and topped with unripe grapes or gooseberries; in Russia they are flavoured with garlic and eaten as *zakuski*, washed down with vodka.

Makes about 2 lb (1 kg)

blackcurrant, cherry or vine leaves
2 lb (1 kg) firm, ridge cucumbers, about 3 inches (7.5 cm) long
1 clove garlic, chopped
1 teaspoon (1×5 ml spoon) black peppercorns
4 sprigs fresh dill
2 tablespoons (2×15 ml spoons) salt

Line the bottom of an earthenware crock or plastic tub with the leaves (this helps to prevent the cucumbers from going soft). Wash the cucumbers well, dry them off, then pack them on top of the leaves with the garlic, peppercorns and dill.

Dissolve the salt in 1 pint (600 ml) water and bring to the boil, then leave to cool. Pour over the cucumbers, making sure that they are covered, and top with a few more leaves. Cover with a plate or board, weight down and set aside for 1 week. The cucumbers are then ready to eat. They can be stored in the fridge, in a plastic container, for 2–3 days provided they are covered with brine.

TOMATOES PICKLED IN BRINE

This recipe can be made with small green tomatoes or ripe cherry tomatoes. They should be roughly the same size.

Makes about 3 lb (1.5 kg)

3 lb (1.5 kg) tomatoes
2 sprigs fresh dill per jar
1 clove garlic chopped
2 teaspoons (2×5 ml spoons) black peppercorns
4 oz (100 g) salt

Wash the tomatoes and dry them carefully. Pack into cleaned, sterilised jars and put 2 sprigs fresh dill into each. Boil 2 pints (1.2 litres) water in a pan and add the chopped garlic, peppercorns and salt. Heat for 10 minutes, then set aside to cool. Pour over the tomatoes, making sure they are completely immersed. Seal the jars well and store for 1 week before opening. Once opened, they will keep for a further week in the fridge.

RUSSIAN PICKLED MUSHROOMS

Most East Europeans have a passion for mushrooms and consume wild fungi with gusto. They also pickle them. This recipe can be used for any kind of wild or cultivated mushroom, although it's best to use only one variety in each batch.

Makes about 1 lb (450 g)

1 lb (450 g) mushrooms
5 fl oz (150 ml) white-wine vinegar
1 tablespoon (1×15 ml spoon) salt
1 teaspoon (1×5 ml spoon) black peppercorns
1 bay leaf
4 cloves

Sort through the mushrooms and discard any that are blemished. Remove the stalks. Wipe with a damp cloth, but don't wash or peel them. Large ones can be cut in half.

Put the vinegar and 10 fl oz (300 ml) water in a large pan. Add the mushrooms and bring quickly to the boil. Put in the salt, peppercorns, bay leaf and cloves and simmer for 10 minutes, stirring occasionally. Remove from the heat, set aside to cool and pack into cleaned sterilised jars. Seal and store for 1 week before opening. The mushrooms will keep well for up to 1 month.

PICKLED AUBERGINES WITH CARROTS

This curious recipe for stuffed pickled aubergines is Bulgarian in origin. It suggests using the strands from the outside of celery sticks as a kind of edible string.

Makes about 2 lb (1 kg)

4 large round aubergines
2 teaspoons (2×5 ml spoons) salt
2 carrots, peeled
4 cloves garlic
strands from celery sticks
1 pint (600 ml) white-wine vinegar

Cut the aubergines in half and scoop out a hole of spongy flesh. Put the halves into salted water and boil for 2 minutes, Drain and leave to cool.

Put the carrots and garlic through a mincer or in a food processor. Stuff the aubergines with this mixture, put the halves together and secure with the stringy strands from the outside of celery sticks. Put the stuffed aubergines into a sterilised wide-mouthed glass jar. Heat up the vinegar and pour hot into the jar, making sure the aubergines are covered. Seal and store for 2 weeks before using. This pickle should be consumed quickly.

TORSHI

Mixed vegetable pickles such as this turn up all over Eastern Europe as well as parts of the Middle East. Use any vegetables in season and aim for plenty of contrast in colours and textures.

Makes about 3 lb (1.5 kg)

3 lb (1.5 kg) mixed vegetables, such as cauliflower, carrots, French beans, different coloured peppers and turnips
4 oz (100 g) salt
1 pint (600 ml) white-wine vinegar
2 cloves garlic
2 fresh red chillies

First prepare the vegetables. Break cauliflowers into florets; peel and cut carrots into strips; top and tail French beans; de-seed and slice peppers into strips; peel and slice turnips into rings. Blanch each vegetable separately for 30 seconds, then drain well and put into a large bowl. Sprinkle with salt, and set aside for a couple of hours.

Drain off any excess moisture, then pack the vegetables into cleaned sterilised jars. Boil the vinegar in a pan for 5 minutes with the garlic and whole chillies. Leave to get cool, then pour over the vegetables. Make sure they are covered, then seal and store for 2 weeks before opening.

HUNGARIAN MIXED SALAD PICKLES

Makes about 2 lb (1 kg)

8 oz (225 g) cucumber, sliced into 1 inch (2.5 cm) rounds
8 oz (225 g) white cabbage, shredded
8 oz (225 g) green tomatoes, whole if small or halved
4 oz (100 g) green pepper, de-seeded and cut into strips
4 oz (100 g) red pepper, de-seeded and cut into strips
1 oz (25 g) salt
5 fl oz (150 ml) white-wine vinegar

Put the cucumber, cabbage, tomatoes and peppers into a large bowl and mix with salt. Cover and leave overnight in a cool place.

Next day, drain off the excess liquid and wash the vegetables well to get rid of the salt. Drain on a cloth. Pack loosely into cleaned, sterilised jars. Boil the vinegar with 10 fl oz (300 ml) water for 10 minutes, then set aside to cool. Pour over the vegetables, making sure that they are covered. Seal and store for 1 week before using. This pickle will keep for up to 1 month in the fridge.

PICKLED PEARS

A very popular Polish pickle that is milder than its English counterparts. It will need to be steam-sealed (see p. 103) if you wish to keep it for more than 1 month. Use firm varieties of pear such as Conference.

Makes about 2 lb (1 kg)

2 lb (1 kg) pears, peeled, cored and cut lengthwise into quarters
1 teaspoon (1×5 ml spoon) cloves
1 small stick cinnamon
rind and juice of ½ lemon
1 oz (25 g) fresh root ginger, peeled and chopped
10 fl oz (300 ml) white-wine vinegar
8 oz (225 g) sugar

Keep the fruit in a bowl of cold water with some lemon juice squeezed into it: this prevents discoloration.

Tie the cloves, cinnamon and lemon rind in a piece of muslin and boil in the vinegar and 5 fl oz (150 ml) water for about 10 minutes. Remove the spice bag and stir in the sugar. When it has dissolved, add the pears (well strained) and simmer until they are tender.

Remove the fruit very carefully and pack into warmed sterilised jars. Bring the syrupy vinegar to the boil and pour hot over the fruit. Cover well, then steam-seal if keeping longer than 1 month.

THE MEDITERRANEAN

Pickling with spices, vinegar, wine and herbs and preservation in oil almost certainly owes its origins to the Roman occupation of the barbarian North some two thousand years ago, so it is hardly surprising there's a powerful pickling tradition throughout the Mediterranean. And it is kept alive by the Italian community living in Britain as well.

We in Britain often seem unaware of the natural foods that are all round us; we are even less comfortable when it comes to using and eating some of these things. Take wild fungi, for example. In Italy they are picked and consumed in vast quantities. Here, we are afraid to touch them. Some Italian Londoners can hardly believe their luck when they find they have, literally, the field to themselves. Antonio Carluccio, of the Neal Street Restaurant in Covent Garden, adores fungi and has a man whose job is to collect as many varieties as possible. He goes to Barnet in North London for 'The Chicken of the Woods' (*Polyporus sulphureus*) and he gets truffles from Dover. Carluccio not only cooks these fungi, he pickles them—

saffron milk caps, wood blewits, tiny puffballs, St George's mushrooms, ceps and many, many more.

He celebrates his particular passion by serving antipasti consisting largely of a glorious array of pickled and preserved things: three or four kinds of fungi, slices of aubergine done in oil and vinegar, sun-dried tomatoes with little pieces of anchovy sandwiched between them.

Throughout the Mediterranean—especially in Italy—pickles are the natural accompaniment to cured meats and salamis: there are vivid colourful peppers, asparagus in oil, tiny gherkins, crinkle-cut carrots, turnips and globe artichokes. Most of them are mildly pickled for immediate consumption. They are a world away from the jars of so-called 'cocktail pickles' sold in our supermarkets.

There is also fruit pickled with sugar and mustard oil—the famous Mostarda di Cremona—and there is still a fondness for pickling small birds in Cyprus. But the most famous pickle of all is the olive. Columella, writing in the first century AD, said you should 'Scald and drain olives, and then place them in a layer in an amphora, covered with a layer of dry salt and a final layer of herbs.' In the sixteenth century they had other ideas: one writer suggested making up a pickle of river water with wine vinegar, orange, citron and lemon juice, as well as the leaves from those trees, plus bay leaves, elder and olive branches and sprigs of wild fennel— to give the olives 'a gentle taste and smell'. Recipes for pickling and preserving olives still vary from region to region and most are jealously guarded family secrets—even though olive pickling is big business.

ITALIAN PICKLED WILD MUSHROOMS

The Italians love pickled wild mushrooms and make use of scores of different varieties. Most common are *porcini*—common ceps (*Boletus edulis*)—but the recipe can be adapted for almost any kind of fleshy edible fungus. It is essential to check a reliable identification guide if you intend to go hunting for wild mushrooms.

Makes about 1 lb (450 g)

1 lb (450 g) edible wild mushrooms, such as ceps
2 oz (50 g) salt
10 fl oz (300 ml) dry white wine
10 fl oz (300 ml) white-wine vinegar

1 teaspoon (1×5 ml spoon) black peppercorns
1 teaspoon (1×5 ml spoon) dried oregano
2 cloves garlic, peeled
2 tablespoon (2×15 ml spoons) olive oil

Sort through the mushrooms, discarding any that are damaged or blemished. Cut off the base of the stalks, if necessary, and wipe with a damp cloth. Blanch the mushrooms in boiling salted water for 5 minutes, then drain. When cold, pack into cleaned, sterilised jars.

Boil the wine and vinegar with the peppercorns, oregano and garlic for 5 minutes. Set aside to cool, then pour over the mushrooms, making sure they are completely covered: the spices and herbs should be included in the pickle. Add the olive oil as a sealing layer and extra flavouring. Cover and store for 1 month before opening. Use up within 3 months.

PICKLED SWEET PEPPERS

This is one of the most colourful of all Mediterranean pickles—particularly if you use red, green and yellow peppers to highlight the effect.

Makes about 1 lb (450 g)

4 sweet peppers of different colours, cored, seeded and halved or cut into
    large pieces
2 sprigs fresh basil per jar
1 dried red chilli (optional) per jar
10 fl oz (300 ml) white-wine vinegar
2 oz (50 g) salt
2 tablespoons (2×15 ml spoons) olive oil

Pack the peppers tightly into cleaned, sterilised jars with the basil and chilli if you want something spicy. Arrange as decoratively as possible to show off the different colours.

Heat 1 pint (600 ml) water with the vinegar and salt in a pan for 5 minutes, until dissolved. Set aside to cool, then pour over the peppers, making sure they are well covered and there aren't any air pockets. Pour over the olive oil to form a sealing layer. Cover the jars well and use within 2 months.

ITALIAN PICKLED AUBERGINES

We sampled a version of this brilliant pickle in Antonio Carluccio's Neal Street Restaurant in London's Covent Garden. He serves it as part of a spectacular antipasti dominated by half-a-dozen different pickled and preserved things, from rare fungi to sun-dried tomatoes. This is not Carluccio's recipe, but it produces excellent results. Some recipes say that the aubergines should be peeled, but it does not seem to be essential.

Makes about 2 lb (1 kg)

4 large aubergines, topped and tailed and sliced
2 tablespoons (2×15 ml spoons) salt
10 fl oz (300 ml) white-wine vinegar
4 cloves garlic, peeled and sliced
1 tablespoon (1×15ml spoon) dried oregano
2 tablespoons (2×15 ml spoons) olive oil

Put the sliced aubergines into a colander and scatter with salt. Mix well, put a plate on top and leave for about 2 hours. Press well to remove excess moisture, then strain and blanch in hot vinegar for 5 minutes. Remove the aubergines and pack into cleaned, sterilised jars, putting slices of garlic and a sprinkling of oregano between the layers.

When the vinegar is cold, pour over the aubergines. Top with a layer of olive oil. Seal well and keep for about 2 weeks before opening. This pickle will keep well for at least 3 months.

PICKLED OLIVES

Fresh green olives are a rarity in England, but it's worth knowing what to do if you happen to procure a bagful.

Makes about 2 lb (1 kg)

2 lb (1 kg) green olives
4 oz (100 g) salt
1 lemon, quartered
1 teaspoon (1×5 ml spoon) dried oregano
1 tablespoon (1×15 ml spoon) chopped fresh thyme
1 garlic, halved

Sort through the olives, throwing out any damaged ones and bits of leaf or stalk. Prick them all over with a pin and put into an earthenware crock or plastic container and cover with cold water. Soak for a week, changing the water every 2 days: this removes the bitterness from the olives. Drain well.

Make up a brine with the salt and 4 pints (2.25 litres) water and pour over the olives, covering them completely. Add the lemon, oregano, thyme and garlic. Cover with a clean wooden board and leave in a cool place for 2 weeks—they are then ready to use and should keep well for several months.

PICKLED ASPARAGUS IN OIL

In this recipe the asparagus is preserved in a mixture of wine, wine vinegar and olive oil. It is quick pickle, almost like a marinade.

Makes about 12 oz (350 g)

1 lb (450 g) asparagus
1 teaspoon (1×5 ml spoon) salt
6 fl oz (180 ml) olive oil
2 fl oz (50 ml) dry white wine
2 fl oz (50 ml) white-wine vinegar

Trim the asparagus, cutting off the woody base of the stems until the sticks are about 6 inches (15 cm) long at the most, making them as even as possible. Put the sticks into a pan of salted water and bring to the boil, then remove from the heat, strain and refresh under cold water. Drain well.

Pack the asparagus carefully in cleaned sterilised jars, keeping the sticks upright. Whisk the olive oil, wine and vinegar in a bowl and pour into the jars, so the asparagus sticks are covered. The pickle can be eaten the same day, and will keep good for up to 1 week in the refrigerator.

SPICED CLEMENTINES

We were scouring the Italian delicatessens around Soho in London, try-ing to glean some information about Italian pickling—with no great suc-cess. In one place, a man browsing through the shelves suddenly spoke up and proclaimed, 'My mother makes pickled clementines in Wales'. That was too good an opportunity to miss, and we pleaded for the recipe. In due course the full details arrived in a letter. So, thanks to Mrs Bosi of Aberdovey for sharing her secrets.

Small clementines are best of all, but any fruit of the tangerine family will do. They go particularly well with pork, poultry and game.

16 small clementines
½ teaspoon (1×2.5 ml spoon) bicarbonate of soda
12 allspice berries
1 cinnamon stick, 2–3 inches (5–7.5 cm) long
½ inch (1 cm) fresh root ginger, peeled
12 cloves
10 fl oz (300 ml) white-wine vinegar
1 lb (450 g) light brown sugar

Wash the clementines and pierce a few holes in the skins with a clean fork. Put them in a large, heavy-bottomed pan, cover with water, add the bicarbonate of soda and boil for 12 minutes.

Place the allspice, cinnamon, ginger and cloves in a piece of muslin and tie with string to make a bag. Add this and the vinegar to the pan and sim-mer for 20 minutes. Remove the spice bag and turn the heat down to low. Add the sugar, stir until dissolved, then bring back to the boil and simmer for a further 20 minutes, covered.

Lift the fruit from the liquid with a slotted spoon and pack carefully into wide-mouthed sterilised jars. Continue to simmer the liquid in the covered pan for a further 10 minutes, set aside to cool slightly, then pour over the fruit, making sure they are completely covered. Seal the jars and store in a cool place. They will remain good for several months.

ESCABECHE

This method of pickling fish originated in Spain and came to England in the eighteenth century, probably by way of the West Indies. The idea is to steep lightly salted and fried fish in a mixture of spiced vinegar and olive oil flavoured with herbs and vegetables. Small fish such as sprats can be pickled whole; others such as mackerel or haddock can be preserved as fillets or chunks. The following recipe is for sprats.

Makes about 1½ lb (750 g)

1 lb (450 g) sprats
milk for coating
plain flour for dusting
olive oil for frying
5 fl oz (150 ml) olive oil
1 carrot, chopped
1 onion, chopped
2 cloves garlic, chopped
2 bay leaves
1 sprig thyme
2 dried chillies
10 fl oz (300 ml) white-wine vinegar

Wash the sprats but leave them whole and ungutted. Dip each fish in milk, then roll in flour to give it a very light coating. Shallow-fry briskly in some of the olive oil for 2–3 minutes on each side. Remove with a slotted spoon and drain well on kitchen paper, then arrange in a shallow ovenproof dish.

Fry the carrot, onion and garlic in olive oil for 2–3 minutes until they are nicely browned. Add the remaining ingredients and cook for 10–15 minutes until the vegetables are soft. Pour the hot pickle over the fish, leave to cool, then put in the refrigerator for 24 hours before eating.

The liquor becomes slightly jellied as it cools. Some recipes, in fact, suggest adding gelatine to produce a kind of pickled fish in aspic.

PICKLED EELS

The eel-breeders of Comacchio in Northern Italy lived in a strange iso-
lated community where life was dictated by the daily business of fish farming and fish curing. According to J. G. Bertram in his book *The Harvest of
the Sea*, 1873, fishermen had already started to dig dykes and build flood
gates to control the flow of water between the lagoon and the Adriatic by
the end of the thirteenth century. This was effective, organised farming of
the waters; in fact the fishermen even regarded the breeding pools as
fields, as if they had been planted with grain seeds.

Much of the work at Comacchio was taken up with cooking and pickling the eels in the vast kitchen. The fish were cut into lengths and roasted
on spits, then packed into barrels with a mixture of salt and vinegar:
always the strongest vinegar and grey rock salt. The barrels were then
sealed and stamped ready for export.

On a small scale this method has been modified: first the eels are lightly
salted, then fried in oil and finally packed in glass jars or stone jugs with a
mixture of weakened vinegar, oil, black peppercorns, mace, bay leaves
and lemon peel. This recipe has echoes of Comacchio, although it is only
intended to keep for a few days.

Makes about 3 lb (1.5 kg)

6 fl oz (175 ml) corn oil
1 lb (450 g) onions, sliced
6 cloves garlic
2 teaspoons (2×5 ml spoons) dried thyme
2 bay leaves
1 teaspoon (1×5 ml spoon) black peppercorns
10 fl oz (300 ml) white-wine vinegar
peel of 1 lemon, cut into strips
2 lb (1 kg) eel, cleaned and cut into 3 inch (7.5 cm) chunks
3 tablespoons (3×15 ml spoons) lemon juice
3 tablespoons (3×15 ml spoons) corn oil

Heat the oil gently in a large pan and add the onions, garlic, thyme, bay
leaves and peppercorns. Fry until the onions are soft and yellow, then
remove from the heat and set aside to cool. Pour in 10 fl oz (300 ml)
water and the vinegar, add the strips of lemon peel, bring to the boil and
simmer for 10 minutes. Set aside to cool.

Rub the eel with lemon juice and set aside for 30 minutes. Heat the oil in a frying pan and add the eel and cook for 5 minutes, gently turning the pieces so they are evenly fried. Transfer to a shallow dish and pour the cold pickle over them. Cover and put into the refrigerator for 24 hours before serving. All this dish needs is some good bread and some good wine.

SQUID PRESERVED IN OIL

In *Italian Food* (Penguin, 1963), Elizabeth David mentions a method of preserving baby squid, or *totani*, in olive oil which she discovered in Anacapri. Huge quantities of these little inkfish are caught in the Bay of Naples at the time of the full moon in August. They are cleaned, cut into rings, then plunged into boiling vinegar for a few minutes. When cold they are packed into jars with fresh oregano and completely covered in olive oil.

The jars are left for at least six weeks, during which time the squid lose the acid flavour imparted by the vinegar, and take up the taste of the olive oil. In Anacapri, these preserved squid are eaten on Christmas Eve.

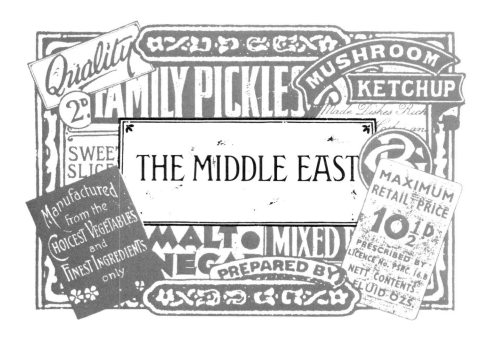

THE MIDDLE EAST

Anyone who has eaten in a Turkish or Lebanese restaurant, with its marvellous array of hot and cold starters, salads and dips will realise that Middle Eastern food has a strong vegetarian bias. Meals often begin with a huge harvest festival of raw vegetables—crisp lettuce, huge beefsteak tomatoes, radishes, spring onions, perfect cucumbers 6 inches long—and a separate bowl of soft, oily black olives. It isn't surprising that pickles have an important part to play in this cuisine.

The mainstays of the diet are cereals, pulses, herbs and vegetables. Fish and meat tend to be extras and are usually handled very simply in grills or stews. Pickles can be used to give a sharp bite to some of these rather bland dishes. The Arabs, Turks, Lebanese, Armenians and Iranians all have a strong tradition of making pickles. It is a family skill and most homes still have *martaban*—jars of pickles ready for eating at any time of the year. There's less need to pickle out of necessity, as different fruits and vegetables can be imported at any time, but pickles still feature in the home, in restaurants, in grocers' shops and even on the street, where vendors sell all kinds of treats. Claudia Roden described this vividly in her marvellous book of Middle Eastern food:

'Squatting on the pavements of busy streets, vendors sell home-made pickled turnips swimming in a pink solution, or aubergines looking fiercely black and shiny in the enormous jars. Passers-by dip their hands in the liquor, searching for the tastiest and largest pieces, and savour them with Arab bread provided by the vendor, soaking it in the pink salt and vinegar solution or seasoned oil. The poor can only afford to dip the bread in the pickling liquor. They sit in the sun, rapturously savouring this modest treat. And when the pickles are finished, the vendor sometimes sells the precious, flavoursome liquor as a sauce for rice.'

(A Book of Middle Eastern Food by Claudia Roden, Nelson 1968)

As well as turnips—which are usually coloured pink with beetroot or red cabbage—there are pickled cauliflowers, cucumbers, chillies, okra, dates, cherries and many more. Usually they are salted or brined, then pickled in a solution of water and vinegar, sometimes flavoured with garlic, dill, chilli, celery leaves and other herbs and spices. Some other pickles, such as lemons, are done in salt and olive oil. Most are not meant to keep for a long time and they are consumed regularly, on their own, as part of a salad or as a tracklement with other dishes.

PICKLED TURNIPS WITH BEETROOT

This is one of the most famous and most ancient of all Middle Eastern pickles. In the Middle Ages it was made with vinegar, honey and herbs, tinged with saffron. These days the colour usually comes from beetroot, which gives the turnips a vivid pinkish hue, highlighting their fibres.

Use either small white turnips cut into halves or quarters, or larger specimens, divided up into neat rectangular blocks.

Makes about 2¼ lb (1 kg)

2 lb (1 kg) turnips, peeled and cut into cubes
4 oz (100 g) raw beetroot, peeled and cut into cubes
2 dried red chillies
2 oz (50 g) salt
10 fl oz (300 ml) white vinegar or white-wine vinegar

Pack the turnips into cleaned, sterilised jars with the beetroot and the chillies.

Put the salt, 1 pint (600 ml) water and vinegar in a saucepan and bring to the boil, stirring until the salt has dissolved. Remove from the heat, then set aside to cool. Pour over the turnips. Cover the jars well and leave in a warm place for 7 days to allow the pickle to penetrate. Transfer to somewhere cool, store and eat within 1 month.

PICKLED CAULIFLOWER

Like pickled turnips (above), this 'white pickle' is often coloured red with beetroot. As an alternative, try using red cabbage, which adds its own texture and flavour. Pack the pickle in layers to highlight the effect: the red cabbage gradually infuses its colour into the cauliflower without over-powering it.

Makes about 1½ lb (750 g)

1 lb (450 g) cauliflower, broken into florets
8 oz (225 g) red cabbage, cored and chopped
2 dried red chillies
2 oz (50 g) salt
10 fl oz (300 ml) white-wine vinegar

Put a layer of cauliflower at the bottom of a large sterilised jar, then add a thinner layer of cabbage chunks, then another layer of cauliflower until the jar is full. Finish with a layer of cauliflower. Slip in a couple of dried chillies.

Boil the salt, wine vinegar and 1 pint (600 ml) water in a saucepan for 5 minutes. Set aside to cool, then pour over the vegetables, making sure they are completely covered. Cover the jar securely and store. This pickle is best eaten within 4–6 weeks.

PICKLED LEMONS IN OIL

The use of paprika in this excellent pickle gives the lemons a beautiful orange colour after a few weeks. Also try this recipe with limes.

Makes about 1¼ lb (600 g)

10 lemons, sliced with pips removed
2 tablespoons (2×15 ml spoons) salt
1 teaspoon (1×5 ml spoon) paprika
10 fl oz (300 ml) groundnut or sunflower oil

Put the lemons into a large colander and mix with salt. Press with a plate and leave overnight, so the lemons lose moisture and start to become soft.

Drain off any excess moisture and begin to pack the lemons in layers in cleaned, sterilised jars, sprinkling a little paprika between the layers. Pour in enough oil to completely cover the lemons. Seal the jars well and allow them to mature for about 3 weeks before opening.

PICKLED ARTICHOKES

There are echoes of Greece and the Mediterranean in this recipe, with its combination of vinegar and olive oil in the pickling mixture. This is a pickle best served as part of a salad or hors d'oeuvre. Choose your globe artichokes when they are at their prime during the summer months.

6 lemons
1 teaspoon (1×5 ml spoon) salt
10 globe artichokes
5 fl oz (150 ml) white-wine vinegar
2 tablespoons (2×15 ml spoons) olive oil

Halve the lemons and squeeze the juice into a bowl. Add salt and mix well. Reserve 1 lemon half for rubbing the artichokes.

Remove the outer leaves of the artichokes and trim the leaves close to the hearts. Cut away the bottom or 'choke', removing all the fibrous hairs. Cut each artichoke in half if it is large. Rub with the half lemon and keep in the salted lemon juice until the vinegar is prepared.

Mix together the vinegar and 5 fl oz (150 ml) water and boil for 5 minutes, then set aside to cool. Drain the artichokes and pack into cleaned, sterilised jars. Add the cold vinegar and top with olive oil. Seal well and store. They will be ready after 2 weeks and will keep well for up to 3 months.

PICKLED ONIONS WITH MINT

Recipes for pickled onions span the globe. They have been used and abused in England, but that is only part of the picture. This version is from the Middle East. It is adapted from a recipe in *Vegetarian Dishes from the Middle East* by Arto der Haroutunian (Century Hutchinson, 1983).

Makes about 1 lb (450 g)

1 lb (450 g) pickling onions, peeled but left whole
2 tablespoons (2×15 ml spoons) salt
4 cloves garlic, finely chopped
2 sprigs fresh mint, finely chopped
1 pint (600 ml) white-wine vinegar

Put the onions into a bowl and sprinkle with salt. Mix the garlic with the mint, then blend this mixture with the salted onions and set aside for 2 hours.

Strain off any excess moisture, then pack the onions into cleaned, sterilised jars. Pour over the cold white-wine vinegar, seal and store until ready. Unlike most English pickled onions, these are ready to eat after 2 weeks.

PICKLED OKRA

Okra—or ladies' fingers—are common in decent supermarkets as well as specialist Indian and Middle Eastern stores. Do not use tinned okra for this pickle—they will produce dismal results.

Makes about 2 lb (1 kg)

2 lb (1 kg) fresh young okra, trimmed
2 fresh red chillies per jar

1 whole clove garlic per jar
2 teaspoons (2×5 ml spoons) black mustard seeds
1 teaspoon (1×5 ml spoon) coriander seeds
2 oz (50 g) salt
1 pint (600 ml) white vinegar

Sort through the okra, wash them well, then blanch in boiling salted water for 2 minutes. Drain well, then refresh under cold water and set aside to cool. Carefully pack into cleaned, sterilised jars. Add 2 whole red chillies and 1 clove garlic to each jar.

Put the mustard seeds, coriander seeds, salt and vinegar into a saucepan, bring to the boil and simmer for 10 minutes. Set aside to cool, then pour into the jars with the spices. Make sure the okra are completely covered. Seal and store for 2 months before opening. This pickle will keep well, as it is preserved in undiluted vinegar. Excellent with stews and cous-cous.

PICKLED DATES

Fresh dates are often preserved in syrup, but they are also turned into a pulpy pickle. It's possible to make this recipe with ordinary dried dates although it is likely to be sweeter and more like a chutney than the original. Some recipes call for *sumak*—the powdered seeds of *Rhus coriaria*— which imparts colour and a distinctive lemon flavour to the pickle. For details of preparing and using tamarind see p. 134.

Makes about 2 lb (1 kg)

8 oz (225 g) dried tamarind
juice of 1 lemon
2 lb (1 kg) dates, stoned and minced or finely chopped
3 cloves garlic, minced or finely chopped
10 fl oz (300 ml) cider vinegar
1 teaspoon (1×5 ml spoon) black peppercorns
1 stick cinnamon, about 2 inches (5 cm) long
pinch grated nutmeg
1 teaspoon (1×5 ml spoon) salt

Put the tamarind into a bowl and cover with cold water, then leave overnight and strain in the normal way. Mix the liquid with the lemon juice.

Add the dates and garlic to the tamarind liquid. Boil the vinegar with the peppercorns and cinnamon for 10 minutes. Set aside to cool, then strain off the vinegar and add to the dates. Add a pinch of nutmeg and season with salt. Reduce the pickle over a low heat for about 10 minutes, or until it looks thick and pulpy. Pack into cleaned, sterilised jars, seal and store for 1 month before opening. This pickle should be eaten within 2 months.

PICKLED CHERRIES

It's worth comparing this recipe with the sweet spicy version of pickled cherries that belongs to the English tradition (see p. 48). The Middle-Eastern style produces sharper, more salty results.

Makes about 2 lb (1 kg)

2 lb (1 kg) cherries
1 teaspoon (1×5 ml spoon) black peppercorns
4 cardamom pods
2 tablespoons (2×15 ml spoons) salt
1 pint (600 ml) white-wine vinegar
1 sprig fresh mint

Sort through the cherries, remove their stalks and throw out any that are over-ripe, bruised or blemished. Put into a bowl with the peppercorns and cardamom. Boil the salt and vinegar in a saucepan for 5 minutes, then leave to cool.

Cover the cherries with cold vinegar and leave in a cool place for 3 days. Strain off the vinegar, re-boil it for a further 5 minutes and leave to cool once more.

Pack the cherries into cleaned, sterilised jars and add the sprig of mint. Pour over the cold vinegar, making sure that the cherries are completely covered. Seal and store for 2 weeks before eating.

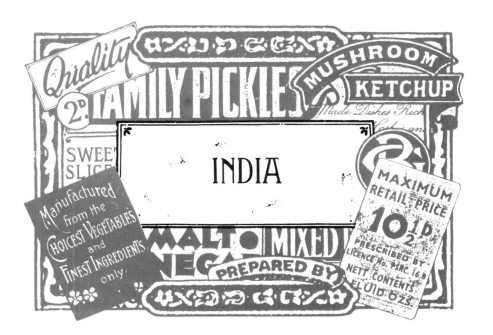

INDIA

'A good supply of home-made pickles and chutneys is the pride of a good cook. With the help of the pickle shelf it is always possible to conjure up a good meal even when it is an impromptu one . . . The art of Indian pickling and preserving is no longer a matter of tickling the palate or preserving food for a later date; it is, in addition, something which decorates the table, swells the pride of the housewife and delights the gourmet.'
(*Shahi Tukre* by Savitri Bhatia, A. H. Wheeler & Co, Allahabad, 1975)

Ever since the first Indian restaurants appeared in London in the late 1950s, we have become familiar with the taste of sour lime pickle and sweet mango chutney. Only now, with the advent of more Indian vegetarian restaurants and special recipes from different regions of the sub-continent can we glimpse the sheer range and variety of Indian pickling.

The problem is that Indian pickles are essentially made in the home, by the family, for the family. Both Saroj Bajpai, married to a mathematics professor in Leicestershire, and Meena Patak, wife of the managing director of Patak's Pickles based near Manchester, remember the rituals and daily business of making pickles in their childhood homes. Mangoes and limes were always pickled in season: limes by the kilo, mangoes by the score. It was a task that involved virtually every member of the family in grinding spices, peeling and stuffing the fruit, packing them in huge jars, tending them and mixing them by hand as they stood in the sun to dry out and mature. Ironically, Meena Patak still makes domestic pickles for her family in Bolton, despite the fact that the family business is based on the daily manufacture of literally tons of pickles and chutneys of every description. The instinct for home-pickling runs very deep.

Indian pickles are full of possibilities: there are hot pickles, sweet pickles, sour pickles, pickles for long keeping, thick chutneys stored for months before eating, quick ones made and eaten the same day as a piquant relish. And the range of ingredients is astonishing: not only the ubiquitous limes and mangoes (of which there are literally hundreds of varieties), but chillies, carrots, aubergines, tamarind, coconuts, guavas, papayas, dates, coriander, garlic, ginger, and even shrimp and partridges.

Pickling in oil is perhaps the most ancient and classic method of preserving fruit and vegetables. It is also the most complicated and time-consuming, as the process involves sun-drying and stuffing with spices. Mustard seed oil was the favourite medium and the pickles were often sweetened with *jaggery* (a kind of molasses). This method of pickling was the great family task in every Indian home, and the results were intended to keep almost indefinitely. But Meena Patak showed us it is possible to scale down this process and make it practical for any household with a taste for the real thing.

Other, so-called 'water pickles', are preserved in a dilute solution of brine, rather like some European pickles. They are sold in large glass jars on street corners in Delhi and other cities. They do not keep for more than a few weeks, and it is said real gourmets don't eat the vegetables at all: they just drink the liquor.

Then there are chutneys—not just the sweet, gluey Major Grey variety that are a hangover from the days of the Raj, but also a whole array of instant chutneys and relishes that can be made in a few minutes with the help of a food processor, and are intended to be eaten the same day. They are so simple to prepare and can transform almost any kind of food, from plain *chapatis* and *roti* to vegetarian snacks such as *samosas*, *bhajias* and *pakoras* to *tandooris* and *tikkas*.

Even when you have mastered all the skills and laid your hands on all the authentic ingredients, you will need something extra to make a perfect Indian pickle. Meena Patak's husband Kirit quotes the example of his grandmother, living in Kenya, who sends an annual gift of home-made hot mango pickle to her grandson every Christmas. 'It really is superb', he says. 'You can always tell when a pickle has been made with love.'

MANGO PICKLE

One of the duties of young English housekeepers in colonial India was the making of pickles. Green mangoes were indispensable and books of the period always supplied several different recipes on the same theme. It was prodigious, time-consuming work, salting and stuffing 50 mangoes at a time, grinding fresh spices and packing huge jars with the pickle. This recipe shows what was involved. It comes from *Indian Cookery for Young Housekeepers* by an Anglo-Indian (the late Mrs J. Bartley), published in Bombay in 1935.

'Fifty mangoes, one and a half pounds of green chillies, one and a half pounds of mustard, one pound of ginger, one pound of garlic, two pounds of sugar, one pound of white salt, two pieces of saffron, one tablespoon of cummin seed, one bottle of vinegar, and one bottle of sweet oil. Pare and wash the mangoes, wipe dry, slice, or cut small; clean the ginger, garlic, and chillies, wash and dry well; cut the chillies rather large, the garlic and ginger finer. Pound saffron finely. Husk the mustard and grind in vinegar. Strew half a pound of salt over the sliced mangoes. When all the ingredients are ready, place a vessel on the fire, pour in the oil and boil, add some curry leaves and cummin seed; fry for two minutes. Add chillies, ginger, garlic, saffron; fry for ten minutes. Add the mangoes, salt, sugar, vinegar; boil for half an hour; add ground mustard. Simmer and cool. Fill into jars. Pickles will not spoil if the ingredients are washed and carefully dried, and sunned for an hour before using. Bottles and jars should be treated in the same way. Always stopper well.'

NORTH INDIAN LIME PICKLE

Apart from mangoes, the most important pickles for any Indian household were limes, which were preserved in countless ways. This scaled-down version, provided by Meena Patak, is easily tackled and needs no great outlay of time or money. Asafoetida is a strong-smelling resin available in block and ground forms, with the ground being the easiest to find. Look for this in Indian shops. For something a little more luxurious, Meena Patak suggests adding walnuts, almonds or cashews to the pickle.

1 tablespoon (1×15 ml spoon) whole fenugreek seeds, soaked in warm
    water for 4–5 hours and drained
½ tablespoon (½×15 ml spoon) ground fenugreek seeds, roasted
2 tablespoons (2×15 ml spoons) chilli powder
¾ tablespoon (¾×15 ml spoon) turmeric
2 tablespoons (2×15 ml spoons) black mustard seeds, roughly ground
3 tablespoons (3×15 ml spoons) salt
12 limes, well rinsed
7 fl oz (200 ml) vegetable oil
10 red chillies
10 cloves
4×1 inch (2.5 cm) sticks cinnamon
1 teaspoon (1×5 ml spoon) ground black pepper
1 tablespoon (1×15 ml spoon) ground asafoetida

Mix the soaked and roasted fenugreek, chilli powder, turmeric, mustard seeds and salt in a large bowl. Make 2 cuts across the top of each lime so they are partially split into segments, taking care not to cut all the way through. Stuff each lime generously with the spice mixture.

Heat the oil in a separate pan and toss in the chillies, cloves, cinnamon, pepper and asafoetida. As they begin to pop, pour the oil and spice mixture over the stuffed limes. Set aside to cool to room temperature before packing in jars. This pickle should be left for 2–3 months before it is eaten.

LIME PICKLE (2)

This is very different to the usual method of pickling limes, because the fruit are actually preserved in lime juice rather than oil. The same recipe can be used for lemons.

Makes about 12 oz (350 g)

1 lb (450 g) limes, sliced or quartered with all seeds removed
2 teaspoons (2×5 ml spoons) salt
1 teaspoon (1×5 ml spoon) turmeric
1 teaspoon (1×5 ml spoon) chilli powder
1 oz (25 g) fresh root ginger, peeled and thinly sliced
5 fl oz (150 ml) fresh lime juice

Sprinkle the limes with salt, turmeric and chilli powder, then mix in the ginger. Pack into jars and pour over the lime juice, making sure that the fruit is covered. Leave in a warm place for a few days, shaking and turning occasionally. After about 1 week, the skins will be tender and the pickle will be ready to eat.

GREEN PEPPER PICKLE

An interesting variation on the theme of stuffing vegetables with spices before pickling them.

2–3 green peppers, slit on 1 side and cored and de-seeded
6–8 oz (175–225 g) fennel seeds
1 pint (600 ml) vegetable oil
1 tablespoon (1×15 ml spoon) dry mustard
1 teaspoon (1×5 ml spoon) chilli powder
1 teaspoon (1×5 ml spoon) salt

Stuff each pepper with the fennel seeds; the peppers should be well filled, and you may need to adjust the quantities depending on their size. Pack the peppers into jars.

Heat the oil in a pan, stir in the mustard, then add the chilli powder and salt. Cook over a very low heat for about 15 minutes. Pour the spiced oil over the peppers and seal the jars. After about 10 days the peppers will be soft and ready for use.

AUBERGINE AND CHILLI PICKLE

The original recipe for this pickle calls for 25 fresh green chillies! Few of us could stand that kind of heat, so this is a slightly toned-down version.

Makes about 1 lb (450 g)

4 small aubergines, sliced
salt
6 green chillies, stems removed
vegetable oil for frying
2 teaspoons (2×5 ml spoons) coriander seeds
1 teaspoon (1×5 ml spoon) cumin seeds
1 oz (25 g) garlic, peeled
1 oz (25 g) fresh root ginger, peeled
10 fl oz (300 ml) malt vinegar
1 teaspoon (1×5 ml spoon) dried red chillies
2 teaspoons (2×5 ml spoons) black mustard seeds
1 stem lemon grass, bruised
1 stick cinnamon
1 tablespoon (1×15 ml spoon) salt

Put the aubergines into a bowl and sprinkle with salt, then set aside for 2 hours. Strain off the bitter juices and pat dry with a cloth. If the chillies are small leave them whole, otherwise chop into pieces. Fry the aubergine slices and chillies in oil until cooked but not browned. Remove from the pan, drain well and set aside.

Grind the coriander and cumin seeds, garlic and ginger with a little vinegar in a pestle and mortar, or use a blender or food processor for the job. Blend with the remaining vinegar until smooth. Add the fried aubergines and chillies, plus the lemon grass, cinnamon stick and salt and stir well. Pack into jars, seal and store until required. This pickle lasts for months.

GREEN MANGO CHUTNEY

Saroj Bajpai instructs English home economics teachers in all aspects of Indian cookery, and has many very quick, simple recipes for pickles and chutneys. This one is from Saroj's hometown of Lucknow in the province of Uttar Pradesh. It goes well with all kinds of snacks and full meals, can be used to stuff *parathas* (shallow-fried breads) and is even good spread on bread and butter.

Kalonji are small, black tear-shaped seeds with an earthy aroma. They are also known as black onion seeds, and are available from Indian shops and markets. Like many chutneys of this type it is ready to eat as soon as it is made, although it will keep in the refrigerator for a few days.

You can make alternative versions of this chutney using sour apples, green rhubarb or even tart gooseberries.

Makes about 12 oz (350 g)

2 teaspoons (2×5 ml spoons) cumin seeds
2 teaspoons (2×5 ml spoons) coriander seeds
1 teaspoon (1×5 ml spoon) fennel seeds
1 teaspoon (1×5 ml spoon) *kalonji*
1 large or 3 small green mangoes
3 fresh green chillies
2 tablespoons (2×15 ml spoons) roughly chopped fresh coriander
3 tablespoons (3×15 ml spoons) roughly chopped fresh mint
3 tablespoons (3×15 ml spoons) soft light brown sugar
juice of 2 limes
1 teaspoon (1×5 ml spoon) salt
extra mango pieces, to garnish

Dry roast the cumin, coriander and fennel and *kalonji* seeds in a heavy-bottomed pan until they start to turn brown and begin to pop. Set aside.

Cut off the stalk end of the mango, which can taste bitter, then peel off the skin with a sharp knife. Pare off the flesh and cut into small pieces. Cut off the stalks from the chillies, but otherwise leave them whole. Put all the ingredients into a blender or food processor with a small amount of water, than blend to a coarse paste. You can vary the texture, but the chutney is best if it is slightly coarse, with whole seeds visible. Spoon into a dish, garnish with a piece of mango and serve.

COCONUT AND CHILLI CHUTNEY

Coconuts in England are little more than fairground props, but in India they are highly prized symbols of prosperity and good fortune. They are also used in many ways in the kitchen. This recipe, supplied by Saroj Bajpai, is from Gujarat in north-west India, and goes well with the vegetarian dishes of that region. It should be eaten soon after making.

Makes about 6 oz (150 g)

1 fresh coconut
2 teaspoons (2×5 ml spoons) cumin seeds
4 tablespoons (4×15 ml spoons) roughly chopped fresh coriander
3 green chillies, stalks removed
1 teaspoon (1×5 ml spoon) soft light brown sugar
juice of 2 limes
1 teaspoon (1×5 ml spoon) salt
lime slices and chopped green chilli, to garnish

Smash the coconut with a hammer, drain off the milk (use this for flavouring curries and soups), then cut away and discard the hard brown skin and cut the flesh into small chunks. Dry-roast the cumin seeds in a heavy-bottomed pan until they are brown.

Put all the ingredients into a blender or food processor, add a small amount of water and blend until you have a paste. Transfer to a dish, garnish with a couple of slices of lime and some chopped green chilli, then serve.

CARROT AND CHILLI PICKLE

Making carrot pickle in India was often a complicated process involving sprinkling carrots with salt, then drying them in the sun for several days, 'removing them before sunset'. They were then pickled in vinegar with whole chillies, ginger and sliced garlic. This recipe, supplied by Meena Patak, is for an instant version that can be made in a few minutes and eaten the same day.

Makes about 1¼ lb (600 g)

1½ tablespoons (1½×15 ml spoons) salt
6 tablespoons (6×15 ml spoons) mustard oil
3 tablespoons (3×15 ml spoons) black mustard seeds, coarsely ground
2 tablespoons (2×15 ml spoons) lemon juice
1 lb (450 g) carrots, cut into 1½ inch (4 cm) strips
4 oz (100 g) long green chillies, cut into thin strips 1½ inch (4 cm) long

Mix together the salt, oil, mustard seeds and lemon juice in a large bowl. Add the carrots and chillies and stir well. The pickle can be served straight away; it will also keep for at least 10 days if stored in an air-tight container in the refrigerator.

CORIANDER CHUTNEY (*KOTEMAR*)

A recipe from *Indian Cookery for Young Housekeepers* by an Anglo-Indian (the late Mrs J. Bartley), published in Bombay in 1935. This pickle can be made fresh each day.

'Grind together one bunch of *kotemar* (coriander) leaves, a slice of fresh coconut, three slices of garlic, a piece of fresh ginger, half an onion, four green chillies, half a pod of tamarind, and a half teaspoon of salt; place the chutney in a saucer and form it into shape. The juice of half a sour lime can be used instead of the tamarind.'

TAMARIND CHUTNEY

Tamarind is one of the essential flavours of Indian cookery, providing a distinctive sharp acidity to many dishes. It is actually a kind of bean, and is normally peeled, seeded and pressed into a lump before being sold. If you buy a lump or packet from an Indian supermarket, it will need to be soaked and sieved before you can use it. This chutney is for long keeping.

Makes about 2 lb (1 kg)

1 lb (450 g) tamarind
8 oz (225 g) sultanas
1½ oz (40 g) dried red chillies
1 oz (25 g) mustard seeds
1 oz (25 g) garlic, peeled
1 oz (25 g) fresh root ginger, peeled
1 pint (600 ml) malt vinegar
1½ lb (750 g) light brown sugar
1 tablespoon (1×15 ml spoon) salt

Put the tamarind into a non-metallic bowl or cup and cover with hot water, then leave overnight. Next day, mash up the pulp with the soaking water and strain through a sieve into a separate non-metallic bowl. Work the pulp through the sieve using a wooden spoon until you are left with only the seeds and fibrous tissue, which can be thrown away. Meanwhile, wash the sultanas and let them plump up in cold water for a couple of hours.

Grind the chillies, mustard seeds, garlic and ginger in a pestle and mortar with a little vinegar. Alternatively, grind them coarsely in a blender or food processor. Heat the remaining vinegar in a pan and add the sugar and salt and stir until dissolved. Add the tamarind pulp and sultanas, bring to the boil and simmer for about 15 minutes until the chutney is smooth and thick. Pack into warm jars, seal and store for 2 months before opening.

KASHMIRI GARLIC CHUTNEY

An exceedingly powerful and potent chutney which tastes brilliant and keeps well for months.

Makes about 2 lb (1 kg)

1 lb (450 g) light brown sugar
1 pint (600 ml) malt vinegar
1 lb (450 g) fresh root ginger, peeled
12 oz (350 g) garlic, peeled
2 oz (50 g) red chillies, stems removed
4 oz (100 g) black mustard seeds

Mix the sugar with enough vinegar to dissolve it. Pound the ginger, garlic, chillies and mustard seeds separately, then blend them together and pound again. Add the remaining vinegar.

Put into a large pan with the dissolved sugar and simmer for about 15 minutes until the chutney is thick, thinning with more vinegar if desired. Allow to cool, pack into jars and store for at least 2 weeks before using.

SWEET MANGO CHUTNEY

Most commercially produced, supermarket versions of this classic chutney are a great disappointment, which is hardly surprising if you look at the ingredients listed on some of the jars. All the more reason for making your own. Use fruit that are just ripe, but still firm: if they are soft or over-ripe the chutney will be very liquid and sloppy.

Makes about 2 lb (1 kg)

1 lb (450 g) ripe mango flesh (about 3 large mangoes)
1 oz (25 g) dried red chillies
2 teaspoons (2×5 ml spoons) mustard seeds
1 oz (25 g) fresh root ginger, peeled
1 oz (25 g) garlic, peeled
10 fl oz (300 ml) white vinegar
1 lb (450 g) sugar
1 teaspoon (1×5 ml spoon) salt

Peel the mangoes, pare off the flesh and cut into small slivers. Discard the stones and weigh the fruit. Grind the chillies, mustard seeds, ginger and garlic with a little vinegar in a pestle and mortar or process in a blender or food processor.

Put the remaining vinegar in a pan, add the mango flesh and sugar and simmer until the fruit is just soft, stirring well. Mash some of the flesh as you stir, but keep some pieces intact for texture. Add the ground spices and salt and continue to simmer for 15–20 minutes until the chutney is thick. Pack into warm jars, seal and use as required. It will keep for 2 to 3 months.

HOT APPLE CHUTNEY

This South Indian recipe was provided by Susie King of Richmond Adult College in Surrey. It makes a good sweet alternative to mango chutney with all kinds of dishes, both meat and vegetarian.

Makes about 2 lb (1 kg)

2 lb (1 kg) cooking apples, peeled, cored and sliced
2 tablespoons (2×15 ml spoons) salt
5 fl oz (150 ml) vegetable oil
1×1 inch (2.5 cm) piece fresh root ginger, peeled and grated
1 whole head of garlic, peeled and finely chopped
2 tablespoons (2×15 ml spoons) white mustard seeds
1 teaspoon (1×5 ml spoon) fenugreek seeds, soaked in water and drained
15 black peppercorns
2 teaspoons (2×5 ml spoons) ground cumin
1 teaspoon (1×5 ml spoon) chilli powder
1 teaspoon (1×5 ml spoon) turmeric
3–4 fresh green chillies, de-seeded and chopped
5 fl oz (150 ml) cider vinegar
4 oz (100 g) sugar

Sprinkle the apples with salt and set aside.

Meanwhile, heat the oil in a pan, add the ginger and garlic and fry gently until just brown. Add the rest of the mustard and fenugreek seeds, peppercorns, cumin, chilli powder, turmeric and chillies and fry for a few minutes, stirring well. Add the apples, vinegar and sugar and continue to simmer over a low heat for about 30 minutes, until the chutney has thickened and the apples are soft and pulpy. Leave to cool, then pack into warmed sterilised jars. This chutney improves greatly with age.

PICKLED BANANAS

An unusual, syrupy pickle that needs delicate handling and acute timing, otherwise the bananas are likely to become soft and pulpy. Serve with curries and cold rice salads.

Makes about 2 lb (1 kg)

1 stick cinnamon
6 cloves
2 blades mace
10 fl oz (300 ml) cider vinegar
8 oz (225 g) light demerara sugar
2 lb (1 kg) bananas, peeled and cut into ½ inch (1 cm) slices

Tie the cinnamon, cloves and mace into a piece of muslin and put into a pan with the vinegar. Add the sugar and stir well until dissolved, then bring to the boil and simmer for 15 minutes.

Add the bananas to the pan. Cook very gently for 5 minutes until they just begin to feel soft. Allow to cool in the syrup, then strain off the liquid, discard the bag of spices and pack the bananas very carefully into jars. Pour the vinegar over the fruit and seal the jars. This will keep for up to 1 month.

PICKLED FISH

A friend from South Africa gave us this recipe with the note that it was an excellent breakfast dish with plenty of bread, and was always eaten in his family on Good Friday—with hot cross buns.

The method of pickling is a mixture of west and east. From Europe—particularly Portugal—comes the style of hot pickling called *escabeche*; from India come the spices. The curry spice mixture varies from family to family, but there's always plenty of 'booster'—fresh cayenne pepper to add fire to the dish.

Use white fish with meaty flesh and a robust flavour: cod and haddock are obvious examples, otherwise choose grey mullet, monkfish or halibut.

Serves 4

1 lb (450 g) white fish, skinned, boned and cut in large cubes
salt and freshly ground black pepper
plain flour for dusting
vegetable oil
2 large onions, sliced
10 fl oz (300 ml) malt vinegar
1 tablespoon (1×15 ml spoon) brown sugar
1 tablespoon (1×15 ml spoon) curry powder

Rub the fish all over with salt and black pepper, then set aside for 1 hour. Dust in the flour and fry in oil until just browned. Lift out the pieces and drain well.

Put the onions into a pan with the vinegar and sugar. Blend the curry powder to a paste with a little water and stir into the pan. Simmer for 10 minutes, stirring well.

Arrange the fish in a shallow dish and pour over the pickle, making sure the pieces are well covered. Cover and leave in the refrigerator for 24 hours before serving. The whole dish—soft fish, crisp onions, fiery sauce—is eaten soaked up with plenty of bread.

THE FAR EAST

Every classic Japanese meal has three crucial ingredients: rice, soup and pickles. That is the Buddhist tradition and it still holds good. In the Japanese home, good manners demand, whatever else may be pushed to the side of the plate, that every last drop of soup, every grain of rice and every scrap of pickle must be eaten. In more lavish banquets, with their seemingly endless succession of dishes, the appearance of this trio signifies that the meal is drawing to its close.

The Japanese take pickling very seriously, and in a corner of countless Japanese kitchens lurks the pickle barrel. This is filled with *nuka* or rice bran, mixed with beer and salt. In it are placed vegetables of every description. The ritual of stirring the pickle barrel isn't some obscure religious activity: it is essential work—leave the barrel unattended and it will go mouldy and the pickles will be lost.

Some Japanese pickles—such as those from the barrel—are for eating within a day or two; others can be kept for a couple of weeks, and there are styles of pickling which produce long-term results. Salt and brine are the most common pickling agents; if vinegar is used at all it will be rice vinegar. There are pickles in Japan that you will find nowhere else—not only salty plums and cucumber and mooli, but burdock root, bracken, and even grasshoppers done in soy and saké. We have sampled these in the course of duty and can pronounce that they are delicious—'half crunchy, half chewy'.

In Thailand, there's also a place for pickles. Dominating everything is the pungent flavour of fermented fish pastes and the fish sauce *nam pla*. The basic Thai meal normally consists of rice and vegetables with one of these sauces, which provide a valuable source of concentrated protein. This style of eating has more to do with poverty and necessity than religion. The Thais produce vast quantities of pickles, in fact most of the jars of pickled ginger and the like in Chinese supermarkets are actually from Thailand. Phillip Harris, who runs the Bahn Thai Restaurant in Soho, London, and has absorbed everything about Thai food and culture, showed us a sample of what the Thais might pickle: four kinds of bamboo shoots, three different types of pickled ginger, whole garlics, little green mangoes, tiny viciously hot green chillies, even onions. Oddest of all are little whole crabs done in salt and brine: 'We just crumble them and use them in a special salad. I don't recommend them to my English customers', he said, 'but the Thais adore them'.

Right across the Far East, from North China to Indonesia, pickles are vital accompaniments to every kind of meal. It isn't surprising that the richness of this tradition, its flavours and ingredients have inspired cooks in the West. Colin Spencer, vegetarian crusader and writer, has done more than most. East meets west in his garden, where mooli and Chinese mustard leaves grow alongside lettuce and tomatoes. And in his kitchen he pickles onions in shoyu, uses rice vinegar instead of malt, wraps little parcels of pickled vegetables in nori (dried seaweed). As a vegetarian he has to be an inventor of pickles; once you take the meat away, you have to devise other ways of making and serving vegetables. And the power and pungency of the flavours attracts him: 'Most vegetarian food is so bland. I like to assault the palate.'

PICKLED GINGER

Pickled ginger is a universal flavouring right across the Far East—especially in China, Japan and Thailand. Some versions are sweet, other harsh and salty; sometimes the ginger is finely cut into slivers, sometimes it is in thick chunks. This recipe is from Japan, where pickled ginger is an essential accompaniment to *sushi* (little morsels of raw fish and other delights on cubes of vinegared rice). It is eaten between mouthfuls as a palate cleanser. Japanese sushi ginger is often pink in colour: originally this was achieved with plum juice; many of today's commercial versions get the same effect with artificial colouring.

Makes about 2 lb (1 kg)

2 lb (1 kg) fresh root ginger
2 oz (50 g) salt
1 pint (600 ml) rice vinegar
4 oz (100 g) soft brown sugar

Wash and scrub the ginger roots, cutting off any skin or flesh that is discoloured or blemished. Using a very sharp knife, cut the ginger into thin slices, diagonally across the root.

Put the ginger into a shallow dish and mix well with salt, then set aside for 2 days.

Drain off any moisture and wash the ginger to get rid of excess salt and pat dry with a cloth, then pack into clean warmed jars. Boil the vinegar and sugar until the syrup is clear, then pour over the ginger, making sure it is covered. Seal and store for 1 week before using. The pickle will keep for several months.

JAPANESE RICE-BRAN PICKLES

Lesley Downer isn't Japanese, but has absorbed the history, culture and cooking of Japan more comprehensively than most English people. She showed us the Japanese ways of pickling and explained that *nuka* (rice bran) pickles are the easiest to make and the most popular. And you don't need to live in Japan to try them!

Traditionally the pickling is done in a wooden barrel or keg with a wooden lid that slips down inside it and a clean heavy stone on top. In practice, a plastic bucket with a close-fitting lid will do just as well. Once you have made the bran mash, you can use it indefinitely—rather like yogurt culture—but you must mix it up well every day, otherwise it will spoil.

Rice bran is normally available from specialist Japanese shops in London, such as Furusato Foods, 67A Camden High Street, London NW1 7JL (Tel: 01-388 4381/3979)—which also supplies by mail order. It is worth checking first, however, before you embark on pickling.

3×650 g bags *nuka* (see above)
1 lb (450 g) sea or rock salt
10 fl oz (300 ml) beer
1 garlic bulb
2 inch (5 cm) strip *kombu* (dried kelp)
assorted vegetables (see below)

Put the *nuka* into the barrel or bucket and mix in the salt and beer. Begin to add water, little by little, mixing with your hands, until the mixture is pasty and has the consistency of unkneaded bread dough. Peel the garlic, leaving the cloves whole. Cut the *kombu* in strips with scissors. Push both the garlic and *kombu* deep into the bran mixture. Cover the barrel and leave in a cool dark place for 2 weeks for the mixture to mature. Each day, you must stir the mixture with your hands.

After 2 weeks you are ready to pickle. Simply bury vegetables in the bran and leave for the length of time indicated below. Any hard vegetables are ideal for this pickle and you can replenish the barrel as produce comes into season.

Cucumber: halve lengthwise, seed and leave in bran for ½ day.
Mooli (Japanese white radish): peel, cut into chunks and leave for 1 day.
Aubergine: halve and leave for 1 day.
Carrot: peel and leave for 1 day.
Turnip: peel and leave for 1 day.
Asparagus: trim and leave for ½ day.

To serve, wash off the *nuka*, pat the vegetables dry and cut artistically into bite-sized pieces. Eat with rice. Any unused pickles can be wrapped in cling film and kept for 2–3 days in the refrigerator.

SALT-PICKLED CHINESE CABBAGE

Another Japanese pickle that is traditionally made in a pickle barrel (p. 139). For small quantities, a glass or earthenware or plastic bowl will do the job just as effectively. Use a plate slightly smaller than the top of the bowl as the lid, and weight it with anything that comes to hand—even a jar of water.

Apart from Chinese cabbage, any firm vegetable can be pickled this way: cucumber—peeled, seeded and sliced lengthwise—is a traditional favourite.

As with the preceding recipe, this was provided by Lesley Downer.

1 Chinese cabbage
rock or sea salt to equal ⅓ weight of cabbage
1×2 inch (5 cm) strip *kombu* (dried kelp)
1 orange, thinly sliced
1 tablespoon (1×15 ml spoon) rice vinegar

Trim the bottom of the cabbage and make 2 deep lengthwise cuts into it, then gently pull the cabbage apart into quarters with your hands. Weigh, wash and pat dry. Weigh out the correct amount of salt. Cut the *kombu* into squares using scissors.

Rub a little salt into the cabbage, kneading it gently into the crevices and folds of the leaves, then pack the cabbage quarters into a bowl, sprinkling each layer with salt and putting a few squares of *kombu* in between. Lay orange slices on top of the cabbage. Mix the vinegar with 4 tablespoons (4×15 ml spoons) water and sprinkle over the top, then cover the mixture with a plate and keep in place with a weight.

Put the bowl in a cool dark place and leave for 2 days. As the brine begins to rise above the cabbage, decrease the weight and adjust the plate. Leave for a further 3–4 days.

To serve, take a quantity of the pickle, gently squeeze out the excess liquid, then cut into bite-sized pieces and eat with rice. The remaining pickle will keep for 2–3 months, covered and left in a cool place in its brine.

JAPANESE MIXED PICKLES

You don't need to have a classic Japanese pickle barrel to make Japanese pickles. There is now a very neat alternative available in most Japanese food shops: it is simply a plastic tub with a screw-down lid that acts as effectively as a wooden slab weighted with a stone.

Any firm vegetables can be used, from cauliflower to mooli, but remember that these are short-term pickles, for eating after a couple of days. They will not keep indefinitely.

Makes about 2 lb (1 kg)

1 cauliflower, divided into florets
1 bulb fennel, outer leaves removed and bulb split into thin wedges
2 carrots, peeled and cut into strips
1 mooli, peeled and cut into strips
3 tablespoons (3×15 ml spoons) salt
10 fl oz (300 ml) rice vinegar
2 oz (50 g) sugar

Bring a saucepan of water to the boil and plunge the cauliflower, fennel, carrots and mooli into it for a maximum of 3 seconds. Remove and drain well. When cold, put the vegetables into a bowl and sprinkle with 2 tablespoons (2×15 ml spoons) salt.

Boil the vinegar with the sugar and remaining salt until dissolved. Remove from the heat and allow to cool. Pack the salted vegetables into the plastic tub and pour over the cold vinegar. Screw down the lid so it presses tightly against the vegetables and leave in a cool place for about 12 hours. The pickled vegetables are then ready to eat and should be consumed within 2–3 days. After that, make up another batch.

TOFU PICKLED IN MISO

The Japanese eat no dairy products and this is their nearest equivalent to a strong ripe cheese. It is very piquant and is usually served in very small quantities, either as it is, or lightly grilled to accompany plain rice.

Fresh tofu (bean curd) is not only sold in oriental stores and supermarkets, but also in some of the better wholefood shops and large supermarkets. It must be the fresh kind: 'longlife' versions will not do. Miso is harder to find. It is actually fermented soybean paste—a brilliant Japanese invention sold only in Japanese shops and a few other specialist food outlets. To make fresh ginger juice, grate freshly peeled root ginger then squeeze through muslin; alternatively use a cunning utensil rather like a sieve without holes to collect the juice. (As with the recipes on pp. 141 and 143, this was provided by Lesley Downer.)

Makes about 2½ lb (1.25 kg)

1½ lb (750 g) fresh tofu, cut into ½ inch (1 cm) slices
1 lb (450 g) red miso
2 tablespoons (2×15 ml spoons) sugar
1 tablespoon (1×15 ml spoon) ginger juice (see above)
1 tablespoon (1×15 ml spoon) saké (Japanese rice wine)
pinch of Japanese seven-spice pepper

Lay the tofu in a single layer on kitchen paper between tea-towels to absorb some of the water. Mash the miso with the remaining ingredients.

Prepare a plastic box with a tight-fitting lid which will comfortably hold the miso mixture and tofu. Fill the container with layers of miso and tofu, beginning and ending with miso. Make sure all sides of each piece of tofu are covered. Cover, wrap the box in cling film and store at the back of the refrigerator.

You can use the pickle the day after you make it, although it is better to leave it for a while—up to 6 months. The longer you leave it, the stronger the flavour becomes.

To use the pickle, simply open the box, scrape off the top layer of miso, and carefully ease out as many slices of tofu as you need, then replace the miso, making sure all remaining pieces of tofu are covered. Cover and return to the refrigerator. Once all the tofu is used up, the remaining miso can be saved and used for any recipe calling for flavoured miso. It is also spectacular spread on bread!

PICKLED GARLIC

A lot of pickles come out of Thailand, but this is surely one of the most delectable. It is chopped up and used with fried noodle dishes, in soups and salads and with fish. It is also marvellous chewed straight from the jar. Phillip Harris of the Bahn Thai Restaurant in Soho in London also recommends chopping up a clove or two and mixing it with scrambled eggs.

Thai garlic is normally pickled as whole bulbs, with skin and stem still intact. Unfortunately most English varieties are too tough for this treatment and you will need to divide them into cloves.

Makes about 8 oz (225 g)

10 garlic bulbs, divided into cloves but unpeeled
1 pint (600 ml) white-wine vinegar
1 teaspoon (1×5 ml spoon) salt
4 oz (100 g) sugar

Boil the vinegar in a pan and add the salt and sugar, then stir until the syrup is smooth and simmering. Drop in the garlic and bring the mixture to the boil and simmer for 5 minutes, then remove from the heat and set aside to cool.

Pack the garlic into clean sterilised jars and pour over the pickle, making sure the cloves are covered. Cover and store. They will be ready to eat after 1 week, but improve with age.

If you find that the skins are still tough, simply peel them off and use the rest.

THAI PICKLED CUCUMBER

Val Hall teaches the ladies of Southwold in Suffolk how to prepare and cook food from the Far East. She also runs a little cottage industry producing all kinds of exotic salad dressings, some of which are virtually pickles. This recipe from Thailand is one of the simplest in the book: it proves that pickle making can be quick and cheap, as well as producing colourful, unexpected results.

This pickle is ready to eat 1 hour after it has been made. It goes well with all kinds of spicy dishes—especially fish—and can be used in salads.

Makes about 6 oz (175 g)

½ cucumber
1 inch (2.5 cm) fresh root ginger, peeled and grated
1 fresh red chilli, stem removed and finely chopped
4 tablespoons (4×15 ml spoons) rice vinegar

Cut the cucumber lengthwise into quarters and slice off the pulpy central core with the pips. Cut each quarter into thin strips (halve these if the cucumber is very large).

Put the cucumber in a bowl with the ginger and chilli and mix well with rice vinegar. Set aside to marinate for 1 hour, then serve.

CUCUMBER PICKLED IN SOY

This is a Chinese recipe. Like many from the Far East, it is an instant dish for eating the same day, and is somewhere between a conventional pickle and a salad in character. As an alternative to cucumber, try using celery: the method is the same except that the celery will need to be blanched in boiling water for 1 minute before it is pickled.

Makes about 1 lb (450 g)

2 cucumbers
1 teaspoon (1×5 ml spoon) salt
2 tablespoons (2×15 ml spoons) sugar
2 tablespoons (2×15 ml spoons) light or dark soy sauce
2 tablespoons (2×15 ml spoons) rice vinegar
1 tablespoon (1×15 ml spoon) sesame oil
1 teaspoon (1×5 ml spoon) sesame seeds

Divide the cucumber lengthwise into quarters, remove the pulpy core and cut the rest into manageable strips. (Sometimes the cucumber is peeled, then cut crossways into round slices; this obviously produces a softer, less crunchy pickle.)

Put the cucumber into a shallow dish and sprinkle with salt. Blend the sugar with the soy sauce and vinegar until it is dissolved, then mix in the sesame oil. Pour over the cucumber, and leave for 1 hour before serving. At the last minute, sprinkle the dish with sesame seeds.

PICKLED RADISHES

A very simple, quick pickle that gives a new twist to the salad radish with its red skin. It is just as effective with slices of mooli (Japanese white radish, sometimes known as daikon).

20 red radishes
1 teaspoon (1×5 ml spoon) salt
1 tablespoon (1×15 ml spoon) light or dark soy sauce
3 tablespoons (3×15 ml spoons) rice vinegar
2 tablespoons (2×15 ml spoons) light brown sugar
2 teaspoons (2×5 ml spoons) sesame oil

Clean the radishes and cut off both ends. Make 2 or 3 small slashes on each one to allow the pickle to infuse, but keep whole. Put into a bowl and sprinkle with salt. Leave for 5 minutes.

Mix the soy sauce and vinegar in a separate bowl. Add the sugar and stir until dissolved. Pour the pickle mixture over the radishes and finally dribble in the sesame oil.

The pickle can be eaten straight away, but will keep for a couple of days in the refrigerator without the radishes losing any of their crispness.

ACHAR (1)

Achar—sometimes spelt acar or atjar—is one of the common names for pickled vegetables throughout the Far East, from Nepal to Indonesia. South-East Asian versions are excellent—crisp, colourful vegetables in a potent sweet chilli sauce, sometimes flavoured with ground peanuts and *blachan* (fermented fish paste). Our favourite is this recipe supplied by Henry Tan of the Equatorial Restaurant, Old Compton Street, London. He tells us it came originally from the Prime Minister of Singapore's mother.

Achar can be served as a starter, or as the essential accompaniment to noodles and rice, spicy fish dishes and curries.

Makes about 3½ lb (1.5 kg)

1 lb (450 g) carrots, peeled and cut in 1½ inch (4 cm) strips
8 oz (225 g) white cabbage, diced
1 lb (450 g) cauliflower, broken into florets
1 large green pepper, de-seeded and cut into 1½ inch (4 cm) strips
1 cucumber, quartered lengthwise, de-seeded and cut into 1½ inch
    (4 cm) strips
2 onions, finely chopped
18 fl oz (500 ml) vegetable oil
1 tablespoon (1×15 ml spoon) chilli powder
1 tablespoon (1×15 ml spoon) paprika
1½ tablespoons (1½×15 ml spoons) turmeric
1 pint (600 ml) white vinegar
1½ lb (750 g) sugar
2 tablespoons (2×15 ml spoons) salt
sesame seeds, to garnish

Blanch each vegetable separately in boiling water for about 1 minute. Drain and set aside to cool.

Put the onions into a blender or food processor with 14 fl oz (400 ml) vegetable oil and blend for 1–2 minutes.

Heat the remaining oil in a large pan and add the puréed onion with the chilli powder, paprika and turmeric. Reduce the heat and simmer for 10 minutes, stirring gently. Add the vinegar and 7 fl oz (200 ml) water and bring to the boil. Stir in the sugar and salt, mix well until dissolved, then remove from the heat and allow to cool. Mix the vegetables and sauce in a large bowl, leave overnight at room temperature.

The achar will keep well in the refrigerator for 3–4 weeks, and can be conveniently stored in a plastic container with a lid. To serve, put some of the vegetables in a shallow dish with a small amount of liquor and sprinkle with sesame seeds.

ACHAR (2)

Makes about 2 lb (1 kg)

1 cucumber, de-seeded and cut into 2 inch (5 cm) strips
4 oz (100 g) French beans, topped and tailed
4 oz (100 g) carrots, chopped
4 oz (100 g) white cabbage, cored and chopped
2 onions, chopped
10 fresh red chillies, stems removed
3 cloves garlic
8 oz (225 g) fresh peanuts, shelled
5 fl oz (150 ml) vegetable oil
2 teaspoons (2×5 ml spoons) turmeric
10 fl oz (300 ml) white vinegar
1 tablespoon (1×15 ml spoon) sugar
1 teaspoon (1×5 ml spoon) salt

Blanch each vegetable separately in boiling water for 30 seconds. Drain and set aside.

Put the onions, chillies and garlic through a coarse mincer. Roast the peanuts in a dry pan on top of the stove until they are brown. Set aside until cool, then pound using a pestle and mortar.

Heat the oil in a large pan or wok. Fry the chilli, onion and garlic mixture with the turmeric for about 5 minutes over a low heat. Remove from the heat, then add the vinegar, sugar and salt. Simmer and stir until the sugar has dissolved. Then blend in the ground peanuts and add the vegetables. Stir until well blended. Leave to cool, then store in a plastic container with a lid. The achar will keep in the refrigerator for up to 2 weeks without spoiling.

PICKLED PINEAPPLE

This quick South-East Asian pickle must be made with fresh pineapple. It is an excellent accompaniment to all kinds of spicy dishes and curries—especially those flavoured with coconut.

Makes about 1½ lb (750 g)

1 fresh pineapple, peeled, cored and coarsely diced
1 clove garlic, chopped
1×1 inch (2.5 cm) piece fresh root ginger, peeled and sliced
2 fresh hot green chillies, de-seeded and finely chopped
1 tablespoon (1×15 ml spoon) white mustard seeds
pinch turmeric
5 fl oz (150 ml) white-wine vinegar or rice vinegar
pinch of salt

Put the garlic, ginger and chillies into a bowl. Add the mustard seeds and turmeric, then stir in the vinegar gradually. Add the chopped pineapple and salt to taste. This pickle can be stored in a bowl or plastic container and kept in the refrigerator for up to 3 days.

INDONESIAN PICKLED FISH

This pickle works well with whole grey mullet or large mackerel, but any firm meaty fish will do. Macadamia nuts are used for flavour and thickening: walnuts are a useful alternative.

1 whole fish, about 8 oz (225 g), gutted and scaled
2 teaspoons (2×5 ml spoons) salt
1 teaspoon (1×5 ml spoon) turmeric
vegetable oil, such as coconut or groundnut
4 macadamia nuts or walnuts
4 fresh hot chillies, de-seeded and cut into strips
6 baby onions or shallots
2 tablespoons (2×15 ml spoons) white vinegar

Make a few slashes through the skin on each side of the fish and rub with salt and turmeric. Heat the oil in a large pan or wok and shallow-fry the fish, turning once or twice, until cooked through and the flesh flakes easily when tested with the tip of a knife. Remove the fish and drain on absorbent paper.

Grind the nuts in a blender or food processor and fry gently in the oil over a low heat for a couple of minutes. Remove from the heat and add the chopped chillies, whole onions, vinegar and 8 fl oz (250 ml) water. Bring to simmering point, then return the fish to the pan. Continue to simmer, stirring until the sauce is thick.

This fish can be eaten hot, straight away, or can be left to cool. It will keep well in the refrigerator for 2–3 days.

CHILLI VINEGAR

This is a very useful standby, particularly if you are fond of Chinese and South-East Asian food. It needs to be quite potent, so adjust the quantities of chillies if necessary. The fieriest results can be obtained by using the tiny fresh green chillies that come from Thailand (colloquially called 'mouse droppings'!).

Makes 1 pint (600 ml)

1 tablespoon (1×15 ml spoon) dried red chillies
1 pint (600 ml) rice vinegar

Put the chillies into a large jar or bottle. Boil the vinegar and pour it hot over the chillies. When the vinegar has cooled, cover the jar, give it a shake and set aside for 2 weeks in a warm place. Then taste it periodically, every few days, until the heat and flavour are right. Strain, re-bottle the vinegar and store it in a cool, dark place.

APPENDIX

SPECIALIST SHOPS

This is a rudimentary list of shops and suppliers selling fruit, vegetables and specialist ingredients for many of the pickles listed in the book: it is not intended to be comprehensive. There is often a great deal of overlap; for instance, Asian grocers often stock West Indian produce, and many Chinese supermarkets have ingredients from Japan and Thailand. Markets in areas where there is a strong immigrant community are always useful; for example, Brixton market in south London for West Indian vegetables.

SCANDINAVIA & NORTHERN EUROPE
Danish Food Centre, 2 Conduit Street, London W1
German Food Centre, 44–46 Knightsbridge, London SW1
Erik Johannson, Metropolitan Wharf, Wapping Wall, London E1
The Swedish Table, 7 Paddington Street, London W1

EASTERN EUROPE

Markovitch, 371 Edgware Road, London W2
Rogg's, 137 Cannon Street Road, London E1

THE MEDITERRANEAN

Greek Food Centre, 12 Inverness Street, London NW1
Valvona and Crolla, 19 Elm Row, Edinburgh 1
I. Camisa & Son, 61 Old Compton Street, London W1
G. Gazzano & Son, 167–169 Farringdon Road, London EC1
Lina Stores, 18 Brewer Street, London W1
Luigi's, 349 Fulham Road, London SW10; 23 Barrett Street, London W1

THE MIDDLE EAST

Food from the Middle East, 36 Upper Berkeley Street, London W2
Kayseri, 47 Newington Green, London N16
Yesil Ada Stores, 115A Stoke Newington Road, London N16
Lazziz Stores, 116 Wilmslow Road, Rusholme, Manchester

INDIA

Ladypool Stores, 158–160 Ladypool Road, Sparkbrook, Birmingham
Indian & Continental Store, 69 Princess Avenue, Hull, Humberside
Sira Cash & Carry, 128 The Broadway, Southall, London
Viniron Traders, 119 Drummond Street, London NW1
Amee Supermarket, Wilmslow Road, Rusholme, Manchester
Rishi Dayanand's Stores, 4 London Road, Tunbridge Wells, Kent

THE FAR EAST

CHINESE

Day-In Supermarket, Wrottesley Street, Birmingham
Wing Yip Supermarket, 96–98 Coventry Street, Birmingham
Nam Kiu Chinese Supermarket, 32–34 Tudor Street, Riverside, Cardiff
Sui Hing Chinese Supermarket, 22–23 Story Street, Hull, Humberside
Wing Lee Hong Supermarket, 6 Edward Street, Leeds, West Yorks
Shun On Chinese Supermarket, 27–35 Berry Street, Liverpool, Merseyside
See Woo Hong, 17–19 Lisle Street, London WC2
Loon Fung Supermarket, 42–44 Gerrard Street, London WC2
Sunki Mini Market, Newport Court, London W1

Wing Yip Supermarket, Oldham Road, Ancoats, Manchester; 45–47 Faulkner Street, Manchester
Woo Sang Supermarket, 19–21 George Street, Manchester
Eastern Pearl Co., 27–31 Fenkle Street, Newcastle-upon-Tyne
Inkap Chinese Supermarket, 148A Mansfield Road, Nottingham

JAPANESE

Furusato Foods, 67A Camden High Street, London NW1
J.A. Centre (Supermarket), 348–356 Regent's Park Road, London NW3
J.A. Centre, 250 Upper Richmond Road, London SW15
Japanese Food Centre, 5 Warwick Street, London W1
N.F.C. Mikado-Ya, 193 Upper Richmond Road, Putney, London SW15
Ninjin, 244 Great Portland Street, London NW1; 140 Brent Street, London NW4
Tokuo-Ya, 20 North End Road, Golders Green, London NW11
Yamato-Ya, 55–57 Church Street, London NW4
Keiko Japanese Centre, 46 Brazenose Street, Manchester 1
Paul's Tofu, 66 Snow Hill Estate, Melton Mowbray, Leics
Miura Foods, 40 Coombe Road, Norbiton, Kingston, Surrey
J.A. Centre, 70 Coney Hall, West Wickham, Kent

SOUTH-EAST ASIA

Cooks Delight, 360–362 High Street, Berkhamsted, Herts
Mustika Rasa, 96 High Street, London SW19

THAI

Matahari, 11–12 Hogarth Place, London SW5; 328 Balham High Road, London SW17; 102 Westbourne Grove, London W2

PRODUCERS AND SUPPLIERS OF PICKLES AND PRESERVES

Most of the producers listed below are small-scale 'cottage industries', although quite a few have well-organised distribution networks. We have not included big names such as Cartwright & Butler. The list is confined to pickles, chutneys and condiments: producers of jams, marmalades and other preserves are outside the scope of this book.

Arran Provisions, The Old Mill, Lamlash, Isle of Arran. Tel: (07706) 606

Burnham Mustard Co., 1 The Quay, Burnham on Crouch, Essex. Tel: (0621) 783868

Charles Gordon Associates, Hoe House, Peaslake, Guildford, Surrey. Tel: (0306) 730776

Clare's Kitchen, Aycote Farm, Rendcomb, Cirencester, Glos. Tel: (0285 83) 555/463

Cumberland Mustard, Sharon Cottage, Slaggyford, Carlisle, Cumbria. Tel: (0498) 81135

Elstone's, 38 Princess Street, Knutsford, Ches. Tel: (0565) 3125

English Provender Co., Aldreth Farm, Aldreth, Ely, Cambs. Tel: (0353) 740069

Farmhouse Fare, Common Farm, Pasturefields, Nr Stafford, Staffs. Tel: (0889) 270209

Fieldfare, 3 Maesgwynne Cottages, Fishguard, Dyfed. Tel: (0348) 874032

Humble Pie, Market Place, Burnham Market, Norfolk. Tel: (0328) 738581

Ridleys County Chandlers, Unit 4, Flitch Industrial Estate, Dunmow, Essex. Tel: (0371) 5744

Tuddy's Garden Shop, Ware House, Ware House Road, Stebbing, Essex. Tel: (037 186) 274

Wendy Brandon, 110 Stanford Avenue, Brighton, Sussex. Tel: (0273) 506868

Wiltshire Tracklements, High Street, Sherston, Wilts. Tel: (0666) 840851

INDEX

Achar, 149–50
Acton, Eliza, 14
Alexander Buds with Fennel, Pickled, 37–8
Apple Chutney:
 Auntie Nita's, 62
 Hot, 136–7
 Uncooked Pear and, 62–3
Apricot Chutney
 Date and, 64
 Orange and, 63
Artichokes, Pickled, 13, 121–2
 Jerusalem, 32–3
Asparagus, Pickled, 30–1
 in Oil, 113
Aubergine(s):
 with Carrots, Pickled, 105–6
 and Chilli Pickle, 130
 Italian Pickled, 112
Auntie Nita's Apple Chutney, 62

Bajpai, Saroj, 125–6, 131
Bananas, Pickled, 137
Bartley, Mrs J., 127, 133
Beef, Spiced, 52–3
Beetroots, Pickled, 32
 Baby, 89, 99
 with Quails' Eggs, 44–5
 with Turnips, 119–20
Bertram, J. G., 116
Bhatia, Savitri, 125
Bismarck Herring, 94–5
Blackcurrant Vinegar, 69

Borthwick, Margaret, 26, 38, 63
Bovik, Alfred, 92–3
Brandied Kumquats, 77

Cabbage:
 Pickled Red, 28–9
 Salt-Pickled Chinese, 143
 Sauerkraut, 89, 97
Carluccio, Antonio, 109–10, 112
Carrot and Chilli Pickle, 133
Carrots with Pickled Aubergines, 105–6
Cauliflower, Pickled, 120
Celery, Pickled, 31
Ceviche, 72, 79–80
Cherries:
 Morello Cherry Relish, 48–9
 Pickled, 124
 Spiced, 48
Chicken, Spiced Pickled, 55
Chilli, 72
 and Aubergine Pickle, 130
 and Carrot Pickle, 133
 and Coconut Chutney, 132
 Vinegar, 152
Chutneys, 13, 16, 22, 126
 Apricot and Date, 64
 Apricot and Orange, 63
 Auntie Nita's Apple, 62
 Coconut and Chilli, 132
 Coriander, 133
 Green Mango, 131
 Green Paw-Paw, 85–6
 Green Tomato, 57–9

Hot Apple, 136–7
Kashmiri Garlic, 135
Lemon and Mustard Seed, 65–6
Peach, 65
Pumpkin, 84–5
Red Tomato, 59
Sweet Mango, 135–6
Tamarind, 134
Uncooked Apple and Pear, 62–3
Clementines, Spiced, 114
Coconut and Chilli Chutney, 132
Coriander Chutney (*Kotemar*), 133
Courgettes, Pickled, 35
Cucumber(s):
    Pickled, 101–4
    Pickled in Brine, 103–4
    Pickled in Soy, 147–8
    Polish Pickled, 103
    Scandinavian Dill, 89, 99–100
    Sour Fermented, 75–6
    Thai Pickled, 147
    Vinegar, Lobsters Pickled in, 52

Damsons, Pickled, 46
Date and Apricot Chutney, 64
Dates, Pickled, 123–4
David, Elizabeth, 53, 117
David Collison's Pickled Shallots with
    Ginger and Garlic, 27
Dill Cucumbers, Scandinavian, 89, 99–
    100
Downer, Lesley, 141, 143, 145

Eels, Pickled, 116–17
Eggs, Pickled, 42–3
    Quails', with Beetroot, 44–5
    Quails', with Rosemary Flowers, 43–4
Elder Shoots, Pickled, 36–7
Elston, Sue, 8, 60, 65
Elstone, Sheila, 8
Equipment, 15–16
Escabeche, 115
Escovitch Fish, 86
Evans, Carole and John, 42, 43
Evelyn, John, 12

Fennel with Pickled Alexander Buds,
    37–8

Fish:
    Ceviche, 72, 79–80
    Escabeche, 115
    Escovitch, 86
    Indonesian Pickled, 151–2
    Pickled, 137–8
Freezer or Ice Box Pickles, 72
French Beans, Pickled, 35–6
Fruits, Pickled, 13
Fungi, Wild, 17–18, 109–10

Gaffelbitar, 92–3
Garlic:
    Kashmiri Garlic Chutney, 135
    Pickled, 146
    with Pickled Shallots, 27
    Vinegar, 68
Ginger, Pickled, 141
Ginger with Pickled Shallots, 27
Glasse, Hannah, 8, 13, 30, 40
Gramma's Pepper Sauce, 81–2
Grapes, Pickled, 47–8
Gravlax (*Gravadlax*), 89, 95–6
Green Pickle, Sweet, 60

Hall, Val, 147
Hamilton, Mayblin, 82, 84, 86
Haroutunian, Arto der, 122
Harris, Phillip, 9, 140, 146
Hartley, Dorothy, 24
Hegarty, Anna, 89, 95
Hegarty, Patricia and John, 9, 45, 48, 50
Herbs and Spices, 18
Herrings, 88–9
    Bismarck, 94–5
    Pickled, 89, 90–2
    Rollmop, 94
    Scandinavian Spiced, 92–3
    Soused, 51
Holles, Tuddy, 67
Horseradish Sauce, 67
Horseradish Vinegar, 68
Hot-Pepper Sauce, 83–4
Hot-Pepper Vinegar, 87
Hungarian Mixed Salad Pickles, 107

Indonesian Pickled Fish, 151–2
Italian Pickled Aubergines, 112

Italian Pickled Wild Mushrooms, 110–11

Japanese Mixed Pickles, 144
Japanese Rice-Bran Pickles, 141–2
Jars and containers, 16
Jerusalem Artichokes, Pickled, 32–3

Kashmiri Garlic Chutney, 135
Klipfish, Scandinavian, 88
Kohlrabi, Pickled, with Saffron, 33
Kumquats, Brandied, 77

Lemon(s):
    and Mustard Seed Chutney, 65–6
    Pickled, 50–1
    Pickled in Oil, 121
Lime Pickle, North Indian, 127–9
Lobsters Pickled in Cucumber Vinegar, 52

Mabey, Richard, Food for Free, 17
Mango Chutney, Green, 131
Mango Chutney, Sweet, 135–6
Mango Pickle, 127
Markham, Gervaise, 12
Marrow Mangoes, 34
Marrow, Sweet-and-Sour Pickled, 73–4
Marsh Samphire, Pickled, 38–9
May, Robert, 12
Melon Pickle, 74–5
Middleton, John, 56
Moore, Dounne, 81–2
Morello Cherry Relish, 48–9
Mostarda di Cremona, 110
Mushrooms:
    Italian Pickled Wild, 110–11
    Pickled Wild, 9, 17–18, 41
    Russian Pickled, 105
Mustard, Whole-Grain, 66
Mustard Seed and Lemon Chutney, 65–6

Nasturtium Seeds, Pickled, 39
Norcott, Sybil, 64
North Indian Lime Pickle, 127–9

Okra, Pickled, 122–3
Olives, Pickled, 110, 112–13
Onions, Pickled, 25
    Cocktail or Pearl, 100

with Mint, 122
Shallots with Ginger and Garlic, 27
Sweet, 26
Orange and Apricot Chutney, 63
Ortiz, Elisabeth Lambert, 83

Patak, Meena and Kirit, 125–6, 127–8
Paw-Paw Chutney, Green, 85–6
Peach Chutney, 65
Peaches, Spiced, 76–7
Pear and Apple Chutney, Uncooked, 62–3
Pears, Pickled, 107–8
Peppers:
    Aubergine and Chilli Pickle, 130
    Carrot and Chilli Pickle, 133
    Chilli Vinegar, 152
    Coconut and Chilli Chutney, 132
    Gramma's Pepper Sauce, 81–2
    Hot-Pepper Sauce, 83–4
    Hot-Pepper Vinegar, 87
    Mandram, 82
    Pickled Chilli, 72
    Pickled Hot, 82–3
    Pickled Sweet, 111
    Picklises, 83
    Sweet Green Pepper Pickle, 129
Phillips, Bernard and Carla, 38, 89, 96
Piccalilli, 13, 61
Picklises, 83
Pigeons, Pickled, 56–7
Pineapple, Pickled, 151
Plums, Pickled, 45–6
Polish Pickled Cucumbers, 103
Pork, Pickled Belly, 54–5
Prunes, Pickled, 47
Pumpkin Chutney, 84–5

Quails' Eggs, Pickled:
    with Beetroot, 44–5
    with Rosemary Flowers, 43–4
Quinces, Pickled, 50

Radish Pods, Pickled, 40
Radishes, Pickled, 148
Raffald, Mrs Elizabeth, 8, 13, 28, 36, 39, 50
Raspberry Vinegar, 70

Red Cabbage, Pickled, 28–9
Redcurrants, Pickled, 49
Reeson, Tim, 9, 33, 35, 44, 55, 72
Relish, 22
  Morello Cherry, 48–9
  Red Tomato, 78–9
  Sweetcorn, 78
Rice-Bran Pickles (Nuka), Japanese, 141–2
Roden, Claudia, 119
Rogg, Barry, 101–2
Rollmop Herring, 94
Rosemary Flowers with Pickled Quails'
  Eggs, 43–4
Rundell, Mrs E., 13, 36
Russian Pickled Mushrooms, 105

Saffron with Pickled Kohlrabi, 33
'Salade' Pickle, 36
Salmon: Gravlax, 89, 95–6
Salt, 18–19
Salt-Pickled Chinese Cabbage, 143
Sauerkraut, 89, 97
Scandinavian Dill Cucumbers, 89, 99–100
Scandinavian Spiced Herrings, 92–3
Shallots with Ginger and Garlic, Pickled,
  27
Smith, Eliza, 13
Soused Herring, 51
Soy Sauce, 36
  Cucumber Pickled in, 147–8
Spencer, Colin, 140
Spiced Beef, 52–3
Spiced Cherries, 48
Spiced Clementines, 114
Spiced Herrings, Scandinavian, 92–3
Spiced Peaches, 76–7

Spiced Pickled Chicken, 55
Squid Preserved in Oil, 117
Stephenson, Victoria, 9, 30, 41, 43
Stockfish, Scandinavian, 88
Sweet-and-Sour Pickled Marrow, 73–4
Sweetcorn Relish, 78

Tamarind, 123
  Chutney, 134
Tan, Henry, 149
Tarragon Vinegar, 69
Thai Pickled Cucumber, 147
Tofu Pickled in Miso, 145
Tomatoes:
  Green Tomato Chutney, 57–9
  Pickled Green, 98
  Pickled in Brine, 104
  Red Tomato Chutney, 59
  Red Tomato Relish, 78–9
Torshi, 106
Tullberg, William, 66
Turnips with Beetroot, Pickled, 119–20

Vinegar, 19–20, 72
  Blackcurrant, 69
  Chilli, 152
  Cucumber, Lobsters Pickled in, 52
  Garlic, 68
  Horseradish, 68
  Hot-Pepper, 87
  Raspberry, 70
  Tarragon, 69

Walnuts, Pickled, 42
'Water' Pickles, 126